Innovations in Education Series
Edited by Robert J. Brown

The Elements of Leadership

What You Should Know

Sarah J. Noonan

Innovations in Education Series, No. 4

A SCARECROWEDUCATION BOOK

The Scarecrow Press, Inc.
Lanham, Maryland, and Oxford
2003

A SCARECROWEDUCATION BOOK

Published in the United States of America
by Scarecrow Press, Inc.
A Member of the Rowman & Littlefield Publishing Group
4501 Forbes Boulevard, Suite 200, Lanham, MD 20706
www.scarecroweducation.com

PO Box 317
Oxford
OX2 9RU, UK

British Library Cataloguing in Publication Information Available

Library of Congress Cataloging-in-Publication Data

Noonan, Sarah J., 1949–
    The elements of leadership : what you should know / Sarah J. Noonan.
        p. cm.—(Innovations in education series ; no. 4)
    Includes bibliographical references and index.
    ISBN 0-8108-4745-0 (Paperback : alk. paper)
    1. School management and organization. 2. Educational leadership. I.
Title. II. Series: Innovations in education (Lanham, Md) ; no. 4.
LB2806.N56 2003
371.2—dc21

                                                        2003000834

∞™ The paper used in this publication meets the minimum requirements of
American National Standard for Information Sciences—Permanence of
Paper for Printed Library Materials, ANSI/NISO Z39.48-1992.
Manufactured in the United States of America.

To my mother, Mary Johnston Noonan,
for your unconditional love, faith, and support.

Contents

Foreword

If you can read only one more book on the subject of leadership, it should be *The Elements of Leadership: What You Should Know*. Although there are literally thousands of books written about the subject of leadership, there are precious few books that pay sufficient attention to the practicality of leadership in our lives. This book differs from other leadership books because not only is it based on research and contemporary leadership theory, but it is also concerned with pragmatic action.

Instead of arguing for one approach or style of leadership (as many books do), author Sarah Noonan successfully argues that it is an advantage to think about leadership in many different ways. She urges aspiring and experienced leaders to think about leadership as broadly as possible to gain a sophisticated perspective about the nature and demands of leadership in many different situations and to identify the types and approaches to leadership that may be useful.

Perhaps one of the most important contributions of this book to the theory and practice of leadership is the *Elements* framework, which allows us to understand leadership in many different contexts. Noonan begins by reminding us that leadership is not just a study of individual efforts and actions, but also a collective activity and a complex phenomenon that has at least five elements. These "elements of leadership" are (1) leaders, (2) members (those who participate in leadership), (3) the situation requiring leadership, (4) the influence of the collective history and life of groups, organizations, and communities, and (5) the impact of change and the future. Complex issues and situations often require very different approaches to leadership if leadership is to be successful.

Noonan defines a leader as any member who consistently acts on behalf and for the benefit of others. This allows more of us to think of ourselves as leaders. She describes how successful leaders build on the following components: (1) their capacity to lead and contribute, (2) their intentions, actions and credibility, and (3) their performance and its effects on others, the situation, and the future. Noonan provides an extremely valuable service by helping leaders to understand the other dimensions of leadership that go beyond the interaction between the leader and members (followers). She expands the idea of situational leadership to incorporate the social and cultural history of groups and the dynamic effects of change and the future. This is a unique and more comprehensive view of leadership.

Applying theory to practical action, Noonan states that our response to problems can be varied and range from deciding to take no action at all, to investigating the root causes and effects of problems using a systemic approach, or to taking immediate action to respond to a crisis. The author writes eloquently about the many dimensions of group, organization, or community history and life, and shows how reading a situation correctly or incorrectly *within the larger context* can result in success or disaster. Perhaps one of her strongest points is that our previous experiences, values, vision of the future, and capacity to deal with change impacts us and affects our leadership.

Some of the most valuable components of this book are the numerous checklists that help leaders examine issues, determine possible strategies, and define what kinds of leadership approaches may prove most successful. Noonan provides a case study of a successful leader who is able to change leadership styles for each aspect of the problem and its solution, showing how being a versatile leader is important. Sometimes it is more appropriate for leaders to be directive while in other stages of the process, being a far more collaborative leader is absolutely essential.

Noonan provides steps and strategies that practicing and aspiring leaders will find immediately helpful in framing and solving leadership challenges. She is masterful in taking illustrations from actual life contexts—providing a realistic approach to dealing with real and complex problems. Because Noonan gives less attention to statistical research models and more attention to a theory of action, experienced and emerging leaders will immediately see how the practical wisdom offered in this book will help them become more successful leaders. The author relates important knowledge about leadership to the practical wisdom of the field, successfully bridging the divide between the theory and practice of leadership. This allows readers access to the everyday wisdom of an experienced leader.

I know that you will find the work of Sarah Noonan, an outstanding educator and leader, to be valuable in your personal and professional life. This book provides a unique yet simple framework to explore leadership in ways that make sense for those actively engaged in leadership work. Instead of finding one best way to lead or identifying a particular leadership style, Noonan urges us to think about what kind of leadership is needed in any situation and what we, as leaders, can offer others as authentic leaders and participants in leadership.

This book is enjoyable to read and is written in a conversational format that helps people see the relevance of each section of the book to their lives. It is the most pragmatic, practical, illustrative and useful study of leadership that people with leadership responsibilities will find. *The Elements of Leadership: What You Should Know* serves as a resource to help solve leadership problems that confront all of us, regardless of what work we do and what titles we carry.

Gilbert Valdez, Ph.D.
Deputy Director
North Central Regional Educational Laboratory

Acknowledgments

I am deeply grateful to many people who have served as mentors and friends to me. First, to my colleagues at the University of St. Thomas, Bob Brown and Tom Fish, I appreciate your encouragement and sponsorship of my work. Next, to my dear departed friend and colleague, Tullio Maranháo, who challenged and guided my thinking on many subjects. A special thanks goes to Tom Koerner and the editorial staff at Scarecrow Press for their work on the manuscript and the final publication of this book.

Thanks to my colleagues in the field for believing in me and offering me opportunities to lead, particularly to Gilbert Valdez, who wrote the Foreword to this book. And thanks to the staff and board members of Teton County Schools and River Falls School District for their endorsement and support.

I also appreciate the lessons that I have learned from all of my students and teachers over the last thirty-two years of my educational career. Many thanks are due to my friends, Mary Carlson and Diane Heacox, for their daily phone calls of encouragement. My mother, Mary, and siblings, Merijean and Patrick, have been lifelong supporters of my dreams—thanks.

Finally, I want to thank my daughters, Jessica, Johanna, and Libby, for their energy, spirit, and love. They are a source of motivation and inspiration to me!

CHAPTER 1

The Elements of Leadership

We are all potential leaders and participants in leadership.

DEFINING LEADERSHIP

Leadership lifts the human spirit. It is not greedy, immoral, unethical, or diminishing, but rather active, caring, constructive, creative, purposeful, playful, and courageous. Leadership is found in homeless shelters and corporate and public offices, on production lines, in schools and places of worship, and inside families. Leadership facilitates the transformational process of change.[1] Leadership ensures the survival of human communities and facilitates the adaptation of people to their environments.[2] Leadership is a spiritual process and releases the spirit or god within us.[3] Leadership is service.[4] Leadership is a visionary process to achieve results.[5] Leadership facilitates learning and develops potential.[6] Can you agree with some or all of the statements above?

You may have already discovered that there are many definitions of leadership and that no single definition satisfies or captures the entire essence of leadership. Each definition adds to our understanding of leadership and helps us to be more aware of what people expect from leaders. It seems impossible to define it! Many philosophers and scholars have examined the role of leaders and leadership in group and community life from the earliest civilizations. Bernard Bass, author of *Bass & Stogdill's Handbook of Leadership*, traces the history, theory, and research related to the study of leadership from early philosophers to contemporary theorists. Bass describes leadership as a "universal phenomenon" and summarizes the many approaches to the study of leadership:

> Leadership has been conceived as the focus of group processes, as a matter of personality, as a matter of inducing compliance, as the exercise of influence, as particular behaviors, as a form of persuasion, as a power relation, as an instrument to achieve goals, as an effect of interaction, as a differentiated role, as an initiation of structure, and as many combinations of these definitions.[7]

Bass encourages students of leadership to define leadership based on the purpose of their search. What is the purpose of *your* search? If you want to learn about leadership and change, try defining leadership as a change process. Think about what you would need to know to be a change agent in your family or workplace. Ronald A. Heifetz defines leadership as a change or adaptive process "to address conflicts in the values people hold, or to diminish the gap between the values people stand for and the reality they face" with the goal of "mobilizing people to learn in new ways and take action."[8] Leaders are expected to take charge during times of great chaos or change—a seemingly permanent condition in organizational and community life.

You might think about leadership as a strategy to provide structure and organization to group work or as a relationship between leaders and members. Using these definitions, what do you need to know? Do you know how to motivate people and organize tasks efficiently? What do you know about building relationships with people or entire communities? There are plenty of resources to help you become more proficient as a leader once you define the term a certain way. Let's consider another example: what do you know about leadership and the future? How can leaders be futurists? Jennifer James states that future leaders need to think in new ways:

> The key is the ability to "think in the future tense." You need to understand how the currents of technological change will affect your life and your work, how economic changes will affect your business and its place in the global market, how demographic and cultural change will alter your self-perception, your perception of others and of human society as a whole.[9]

What is the role of leaders and members in addressing the challenges of the future? What are the strategies that futurists use to lead communities? Instead of searching for the best definition of leadership, try collecting many different definitions. Here's another example: the goal of leadership during a crisis is to restore order and facilitate healing. How do organizing and healing fit into your definition of leadership? Can you see yourself as an organizer, strategist, and healer during a crisis?

YOUR PERSONAL DEFINITION OF LEADERSHIP

It is an *advantage* to think about leadership in many different ways. This allows you to build a richer picture of leadership and find many ways to contribute. I have written at least fifty definitions of leadership; they are all correct and inadequate! You may want to consider writing a personal definition of leadership that reflects some of your ideas about leadership and fits with your life and work.

Here is my personal working definition of leadership: *leadership develops potential and builds community*. One way to develop potential is to help people identify their talents and encourage them to use those talents as often as possible.[10] If you believe in the potential of others, you soon become an expert talent scout and favor more flexible and creative work environments. The language and actions of coaching can help to guide your thinking about talent development. Talent-focused leaders plan a winning season by selecting and developing talent. My personal definition fits with my life. I am a teacher, executive coach, and mentor to students and leaders in the field. What is your personal definition of leadership? How does it fit with your life?

Try describing some of the important roles of leaders as they relate to your definition. Does your definition help you visualize your leadership in action and point the way to your future development? Your personal definition of leadership is like your personal mission statement; it should influence the direction of your life and serve as a standard by which to judge your actions. You can continually expand your definition of leadership based on new learning. You may want to start a collection of leadership definitions to focus your attention on the various aspects of leadership that interest you.

Mature leaders continually revise and expand their definitions of leadership and their knowledge and skill set for leading. These examples illustrate the importance and usefulness of thinking broadly about leadership. If you conducted an Internet search on Amazon.com, an online bookseller, you would discover over 12,000 current titles associated with the subject heading "leadership."[11] Defining leadership in many different ways can help you to understand leadership as a phenomenon.

The study of leadership involves the study of leaders, what they do, and how leaders and followers influence each other. But there is more to leadership than leaders' and followers' actions. There are also situations requiring leadership; the collective history of group, organizational, and community life and their members; and the impact of change and the future. These combined factors make up the Elements of Leadership, a framework to help you understand the various factors or elements influencing and affecting leadership.

THE ELEMENTS OF LEADERSHIP—A FRAMEWORK

The elements of leadership are (1) leaders, (2) members, (3) the situation requiring action, (4) the group, organization, or community where leadership occurs, and (5) change and the future (see figure 1). The first element, the "leader," is any member who consistently acts on behalf of and for the benefit of others. The second element, the "member," is any individual who belongs to a group and participates in acts of leadership. Leaders and members together identify problems, create solutions, participate in decisions and actions, and accomplish results.

The third element, the "situation," refers to the unique characteristics and task requirements of any novel situation where acts of leadership and participation are needed to solve problems or mine opportunities. Leaders and members uncover the unique requirements of situations and capitalize on the talents and collective knowledge of the membership to identify strategies and take action.

The fourth element, "group, organization, or community," refers to the history and present experience of people as members of social groups. Knowledge of group history and life allows us to discover the underlying causes, sources, and meaning of any situation. It allows us

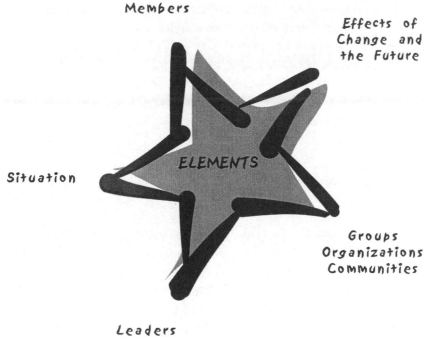

Members

Effects of
Change and
the Future

Situation

ELEMENTS

Groups
Organizations
Communities

Leaders

Figure 1

to predict and examine the motivations and intentions of individuals and groups, anticipate the potential response and impact of proposed actions, discover the viable and eliminate the unworkable directions or strategies for development and change, and evaluate the costs, effort, and impact of leadership.

The fifth and last element, "change and the future," refers to the adjustment of people to change and its effects and the anticipated and actual effects of an innovation on the immediate and long-term future of the group, organization, and community as nested systems. Stepping back from the immediate "situation," the fifth element encourages a probing analysis of what happens under the surface when change occurs, impacting people, culture, and systems.

The Elements of Leadership vary in their influence and degree of importance based on the many different perspectives that are possible and the range of view. If you think about leadership as a dynamic system with many different elements, you can increase your understanding of what happens by considering the interaction and intersection of the Elements and their relative influences and effects. This knowledge can help you be a more effective and strategic leader.

The Elements of Leadership: What You Should Know challenges you to go beyond the narrow view of leadership as consisting primarily of the actions or effects of a single individual or even fundamentally as a relationship between leaders and followers—it is that and more! Let's examine the Elements and the attack on the World Trade Center that took place on 9-11-01.

THE ELEMENTS OF LEADERSHIP AND THE ATTACK ON THE WORLD TRADE CENTER

There were many acts of leadership exhibited during the World Trade Center (WTC) attack. One element of leadership is the "leader." While there were many leaders during this crisis, Mayor Rudolph Giuliani was a visible symbol and an authentic leader of the crisis centered at Ground Zero. Giuliani had a remarkable understanding of what people need and want from leaders during a crisis and delivered it with passion and skill.

During a crisis, people expect leaders to define reality, contain the crisis, and restore order. Giuliani established a chain of command and put into motion a systematic approach to dealing with the victims, the survivors, and the site. Effective crisis leaders are great communicators and empathetic and hopeful leaders. Giuliani likened the experience of the WTC attack to the bombing of London. He studied Winston Churchill's actions and wanted to inspire people to survive the crisis and prevail. In this case, as a leader, Mayor Giuliani made a significant difference in the outcome of the WTC attack and was therefore a critical element of leadership.

While elected and appointed leaders were significant participants in leadership, the spontaneous leadership of "followers or members" was another significant element. Workers and volunteers rescued victims, buried the dead, provided food, and did whatever was needed. These participants in leadership included emergency-management personnel, volunteers, clergy, and citizens. They participated in leadership because of their membership in groups, organizations, and communities. Family members searched for loved ones. Emergency-management personnel initiated rescue efforts. New York construction workers grabbed tools and dug through the rubble. Much of this work was completed without the direction of leaders. The participation of "members" is another element of leadership.

The collective effect of the unplanned actions of people during the crisis cannot be attributed to the actions of a single leader. Did Mayor Giuliani by his office or position direct the response to the crisis, or did the members lead themselves when they determined what was needed? Clearly both positions are true.

While leaders and members are critical elements in understanding leadership, yet another element of leadership is the "situation" itself. The WTC attack was a crisis. A crisis is a threat to survival, and the factors associated with crises influence the decisions and actions of leaders, members, groups, organizations, and communities. A crisis creates opportunity for leadership and dictates a pattern of action. The goal of crisis management is to contain the damage, restore stability, and learn from the situation.

Does the leader influence what takes place or merely respond to the dynamics of yet another element of leadership called the situation? How much does the event or situation explain what is described as leadership? The nature of a crisis, including the unfolding of the event and expectations of leaders and members during a crisis, follows a predictable pattern, which we can understand. Clearly the situation is another important element of leadership.

The WTC attack was not just an attack on people working at the WTC or the destruction of a building; it was also an attack on American culture and the people and government of the United States. The WTC attack must be viewed in the context of the international stage, where the roots of the conflict can be located in the history of religious and cultural fanaticism, war and foreign policy, poverty, the insane and unspeakable history and horror of terrorism, and more. Group, organizational, and community life is an element of leadership because it locates the sources of problems and opportunities and explains our response to them. Knowledge about the history and status of various groups, organizations, and communities is another important element because it expands our ideas about the setting where leadership occurs and the anticipated effects of proposed or actual decisions and actions.

The horrible costs of the WTC attack, including the human effort and capital resources required to contain the crisis and the secondary crises that followed, comprise yet another element of leadership—the effects of change and the future. How much will the WTC attack affect our thoughts about the future? The fifth element of leadership, the effects of "change and the future," incorporates knowledge about the past and its effects and also about the future—what we anticipate may happen as a result of our experience and the next-level challenges that are unforeseen.

It is easy to trace the impact of the WTC attack. The Department of Homeland Security was created to address threats to security in our country. Legislation favoring security concerns over the right to privacy was approved by Congress to increase the power of authorities in tracking down potential terrorists. These measures are some of the cascading effects of the events of 9-11-01.

Future concerns following the events of 9-11-01 dominate the landscape and are a critical element in explaining and interpreting some of the decisions and actions of leadership in response to the attack. So, how can we explain leadership in this tragic event? What element best explains the nature and process of leadership? Was it the actions of Giuliani, the emergency personnel, or the people of New York? Was it the circumstances surrounding the WTC attack and the knowledge that there would be future threats to homeland security? Was it the failure of the world community to establish conditions where peace, not war, thrives?

These questions help us to focus on the relative importance of the Elements of Leadership and the WTC crisis. No single element explains what happens when leadership occurs, but rather a combination of elements and their effects describes leadership. Instead of trying to eliminate facets and explain the crisis using a limited definition of leadership, the Elements outlined in this book allow us to look at the challenges of leadership and the WTC attack in a more complete way.

Applying the Elements to many different situations or events can help you become more strategic in understanding what happens when leadership occurs and what elements or factors are likely to be affected when leaders take action. Because leadership is a complex phenomenon, the study of philosophy, sociology, political science, anthropology, and other disciplines can increase your understanding of the nature and history of human groups and leadership. The Elements presented here can also serve as the scaffolding to support your knowledge from many disciplines.

The study of leadership is the study of our development and progress as humans and our membership in communities. It cannot be defined or captured in any theory or publication (including this one!). It is about people, power, poverty, progress, oppression, change, technology, beliefs, values, and ethics. It is about humanity and culture, social change, and revolution. It is about our past, present, and future.

Radical and rapid cultural and social changes have altered our view of what we want from leaders, of the "leader's work," and of the nature of leadership. The Elements reveal the complexity of leadership through the simplicity of one model; they can help you increase your awareness and raise your consciousness about your own leadership and the collective experience and participation of others in leadership. You can learn to become a more successful leader and member by using the Elements as a lens to understand and as a tool to locate the challenges and opportunities of leadership in many different settings.

The goal of *The Elements of Leadership: What You Should Know* is not to offer a surefire leadership recipe or supply cookbook solutions to the problems in human groups and communities. There is far too much complexity and uncertainty in our lives and the study of leadership! If it were simple, you wouldn't be reading this book. The Elements offer you a structure to organize your thinking and knowledge about leadership by figuring out which of the elements of leadership are emphasized in various definitions or conceptualizations of leadership. The Elements of Leadership is also an analytical and creative thinking tool that helps you dissect, deconstruct, analyze, interpret, predict, or explain leadership in many different settings.

This is a simple book about a complex subject. *The Elements of Leadership* introduces you to the approximate territory of leadership but provides no map for the "one" best way to think about leadership, except that leadership is always defined as a moral activity. *Leadership is ethical action.* The purpose of leadership is to elevate the human condition. The references to leaders and leadership throughout this book assume this ethical definition of leadership.

My friend and colleague Dr. Tom Fish and I were evaluating a student project, and he offered a summarizing statement about unethical leadership related to the student's work. He said, "Evil is circular!" I laughed and agreed. Later I thought about his comment and related it to leadership—leadership is circular too! The more leadership is created, the more it returns to develop potential and build community. As I have already argued, it is useful to think of many definitions and models of leadership to increase your understanding and development rather than searching for the best definition and model (even this one).

Dr. Kathleen Allen, a colleague and friend, discussed an idea about leadership with me. She said, "Sarah, what we really need is not more leaders, but more leadership!" I challenge you to think about what this means as you expand your knowledge and skills as a participant in and student of leadership. The next chapter begins with a discussion of the leader as one element of leadership.

NOTES

1. See Michael Fullan, *Leading in a Culture of Change* (San Francisco: Jossey-Bass, 2001) for information on facilitating change in business and education.

2. A definition of leadership as an adaptive process and as a process to resolve conflicts in communities can be found in Ronald A. Heifetz, *Leadership without Easy Answers* (Cambridge, Mass.: Harvard University Press, 1994).

3. The role of spirituality in work life and leadership can be found in Jay A. Conger et al., *Spirit at Work* (San Francisco: Jossey-Bass, 1994) and Robert Terry, *Seven Zones for Leadership: Acting Authentically in Stability and Chaos* (Palo Alto, Calif.: Davies-Black Publishing, 2001).

4. Robert Greenleaf, *Servant Leadership: A Journey into the Nature of Legitimate Power and Greatness* (New York: Paulist Press, 1977).

5. See Warren Bennis and Burt Nanus, *Leaders: The Strategies for Taking Charge* (Harper & Row Publishers, 1985) for a summary of a study of ninety executive leaders distinguished from managers by their vision and tenacity related to goals and other factors.

6. See Max De Pree, *Leading without Power: Finding Hope in Serving Community* (San Francisco: Jossey-Bass, 1997) for strategies to develop individual and organizational potential.

7. Bernard Bass, *Bass & Stogdill's Handbook of Leadership: Theory, Research, and Managerial Applications*, 3rd ed. (New York: The Free Press, 1990), 19.

8. Heifetz, *Leadership without Easy Answers*, 22.

9. Jennifer James, *Thinking in the Future Tense: Leadership Skills for a New Age* (New York: Simon & Schuster, 1996), 24.

10. See Marcus Buckingham and Don Clifton, *Now, Discover Your Strengths* (New York: The Free Press, 2001) and Donald Clifton and Paula Nelson, *Soar with Your Strengths* (New York: Dell Publishing, 1992) for a discussion of strengths and talent development.

11. See www.amazon.com; enter the keyword *leadership* in the subject search window.

CHAPTER 2

Leaders

The potential for leaders to make a positive difference is ever present.

DEFINING LEADERSHIP

We look everywhere for ideas about how to be leaders. There are hundreds of books on the subject of leadership, ranging from how we can learn most of what we need to know about business (and executive leadership) by playing games, outsmarting the competition, or applying the strategies of winning football coaches. Each of these resources has the potential to offer us some "practical wisdom" about being a leader and help us to think about leaders and leadership in different ways. Here's a little story about Alexander the Great and his experience as a leader. See if you agree with the advice offered in this story:

> Alexander the Great prepared for his eventual rise to leadership with an ambitious educational program. Tutored by Aristotle, he studied the subjects of science, geography, philosophy, and literature. Alexander also learned about military strategy and politics. These same subjects are found in many leadership preparation programs, but we call them by new names: Finance 101, Strategic Planning, Technology and Change, Transnational Corporations, and the like. *If you want to be a leader, study hard!*
> When Alexander's father, King Philip of Macedonia, was murdered, Alexander claimed the throne and continued his father's war with Asia. Rivals for the throne soon challenged Alexander. *He overcame these*

threats with strategy and cunning. Even after Alexander established himself as king, rebellion broke out in some regions when it was rumored that Alexander had been killed in a battle. *Visibility is an important asset of leadership. When it becomes obvious to followers and would-be kings that the leader no longer has power by position or persuasion (and can no longer hold the throne), the leader had better watch his or her back!*

Alexander journeyed in 333 B.C. to Gordium, where he united his armies. The area of Gordium was named after Gordius, a poor peasant who became king when he entered town in an oxcart. According to Greek legend, Gordius was so grateful for his good fortune that he dedicated his oxcart to the god Zeus and tied it up with an unusual knot. *Pay homage to your supporters and tie up your assets!*

An oracle prophesized that anyone who could successfully untie Gordius's knot would become the ruler of Asia. Alexander went to the square to take on this knotty challenge (ouch!). Apparently the Gordian knot had ends that were folded inside the knot and could not be detected. After trying unsuccessfully to untie the Gordian knot, Alexander drew his sword and cut it. This fulfilled the oracle's prophecy and earned Alexander the right to become the ruler of Asia. *Alexander met the challenge by thinking about the problem and the solution in a novel way and took decisive action to solve it.* Alexander's creativity and riches might be compared to corporate entrepreneurs who have acquired tremendous wealth from their creative thinking. Bill Gates, founder of Microsoft, is a living example. Good ideas can yield fantastic results.

LEADERS AS WARRIOR-KINGS—AN OLD FRAME

The underlying theme of some of the most popular books on leaders and leadership is that leaders are warriors, the organization is the battlefield, and the enemy is the competitor (or those inside the organization who are in the leader's way). Leaders, as warrior-kings, are engaged in a battle for members' participation. I'm sure that sometimes it feels that way! A highly political environment can feel like a battlefield, and sometimes it feels safer to wear some armor to work. Militaristic models might work on the battlefield, but this is an old "frame" for thinking about leadership. Warlike behavior just doesn't work very effectively with adults in most organizational and community environments.

Understanding your role as a leader and as a member is central to your success as a leader. Alexander's lessons are simple (and sometimes true), but it takes intelligence and experience to figure out whether the advice applies in any situation. For example, when is it a good idea to address a threat with a covert strategy and cunning and when is it simply a good idea to call a halt to the threat, accept defeat, and lay down your arms? Sometimes not engaging in the battle is the right answer. Your central role as a leader is to identify the important functions of leadership as an activity and to identify what you can bring to the role of leader that is useful to others.

WHAT LEADERS (AND MEMBERS) DO

Leadership is about what leaders and members do together. The leader is a critical element of leadership because leaders initiate, convene, and orchestrate the leadership process with members to accomplish goals. The role of leaders is to "create a space where dialogue can happen, where truth can be discovered, and where day-to-day decisions can be made, [so that] he or she can quit being the leader and start convening the process in which the activity of leadership happens."[1] This process does not negate what a leader with high levels of expertise, energy, and experience can bring to the table as a contributor. *The leader in you consists of (1) your capacity to lead and contribute, (2) your intentions, actions, and credibility, and (3) your performance and its effects on others, the situation, and the future.*

You leadership capacity is what you can offer to others as a resource in any given situation and consists of your knowledge, skills, and personal qualities. As the convener of the process, your skills in process facilitation, relationship building, and interpersonal and group communication are important assets. Your experience in leading, contributing, and learning shapes you and your capacity to lead and serve. Your life experience, education, service, and past performance are some of the building blocks of that capacity. While your capacity is made up of what you can do, your leadership potential consists of your undeveloped talents and opportunities for growth from new learning.

Try taking the "elevator test"—can you describe why you want to be a leader before you reach the third floor? In simple words, what motivates you? What do you intend to do with your life? Your intentions consist of your underlying ethics, values, principles, beliefs, and passions as the motivating source of your work with others. Your actions are what you do in your personal and public life to deliver on your intentions. The measure of the congruence of intention and action is credibility. Credibility is the measure of your constancy and faithfulness to your espoused values. Although your intentions are not visible, they are often detected or inferred from your actions. When someone donates money or service, we assume kindness, empathy, or an ethic of care. Credible leaders align their espoused values with their actions.

Finally, your performance is evaluated based on the merits of the process and its measurable effects and outcomes—the way that others respond to the call for participation and how they evaluate the costs associated with participation and the results. Were the goals accomplished? Was the process productive? Were the talents of others fully used to accomplish the outcomes? What was the net effect of the leadership process: affirming or destructive?

Your net capacity as a leader is based on your individual expertise and your willingness and ability to work with others. Leadership requires a high level of situational knowledge and tactical skill. Leaders initiate processes to identify and solve problems and locate and mine opportunities for the common good of the membership. The leader's work is varied and involves organizing tasks and providing structure to accomplish work, establishing priorities, facilitating group interaction and organizational learning, ensuring consistency and maintaining stability, and engaging others in change and planning for the future.

Effective leaders work with others to accomplish goals. You might think of leadership as both a personal strategy and an organizational process to take action and achieve goals. Leadership occurs when leaders and members collaborate to accomplish the following:

1. Develop a shared purpose, mission, and vision for the future
2. Define the current reality
3. Investigate the situation and context requiring action
4. Identify a direction, strategy, or goal and take action
5. Assess and evaluate the effects of collective actions on quality, performance, accomplishment, and the future

The leadership process is similar to a problem-solving process. It is arduous and messy. Leaders facilitate the process of problem solving by locating opportunity in problems and identifying strategies for creative and productive change. This process often involves going through some or all of the steps several times before the problem or opportunity is fully understood.

Leaders unleash the creative potential of people by facilitating effective meetings and encouraging the individual and group development of creative-thinking processes.[2] Leaders often serve as creative or artistic directors of a community. Images of workers as artists come to mind. How can you develop your ability to think creatively and facilitate the creative process? What is your current capacity to lead and work with people engaged in problem-solving activities? How is leadership a creative process?

Effective leaders are proactive and concentrate on the health and vitality of the organization and the future. Effective leaders focus on the vision defined as "*a realistic, credible, attractive future for your organization.*"[3] According to Burt Nanus, the right vision (1) attracts commitment and energizes people, (2) creates meaning in workers' lives, (3) establishes a standard of excellence, and (4) bridges the present with the future.[4] What is your knowledge of vision-building processes?

How do leaders work with members to ensure the stability of an organization over time? Having a vision is important, and knowing when it is necessary to change that vision can be even more important. How do you identify the situational factors in your internal and external environments that necessitate change? What do you do when vision isn't enough? Leading is both planned and spontaneous:

> You may have an overarching vision, clear, orienting values, and even a strategic plan, but what you actually do from moment to moment cannot be scripted. To be effective, you must respond to what's happening.[5]

Effective leaders continue to develop their capacity to lead and contribute. The actions of leaders are varied and situational. You become a seasoned leader because of the challenges in your environment and what you learn. Effective leaders develop a high level of expertise and a solid ability to work with people. Your capacity (and competence) to work successfully in many different situations is one factor in your success as a leader. Another factor is your ability to persuade others to participate and support your leadership. Participation and support are the gifts of members. Member participation depends on the actions you propose, your intentions and actions, and your leadership track record.

Although we expect leaders to be competent, we also expect them to be moral. You won't lose support as a leader if you admit that you don't know what to do or make an honest mistake (unless you are hopelessly incompetent!), but you will lose support if you do the wrong thing and lose credibility. We expect leaders to have some of the right stuff to lead—including credibility, honesty, and caring. What qualities do you think leaders should possess to inspire your participation?

THE QUALITIES OF LEADERS

The qualities of leaders are the enduring values and behaviors that define them. Numerous surveys have been conducted to identify the important qualities of leaders. Qualities such as trustworthiness, honesty, integrity, fairness, and a high moral character are frequently described. *Personal traits or qualities do not adequately explain the success or failure of leaders.* However, the leader's qualities do have some influence on the process and the level of participation of others, particularly when these qualities inspire commitment to the larger mission and goals of the organization.

In some cases, leadership qualities or traits are an entrance requirement to leadership. You need some qualities as a precondition to lead, along with a reasonable plan and process to enlist the support and participation of others. Qualities may be part of your personal success in certain situations. According to Bass, your traits and areas of competence may be a fit in some situations requiring leadership and explain some of the results.[6]

What qualities are unique to you? I'd like to share a story about a young woman, Johanna Smith, who lost her sight in 1992, and relate this story to the qualities of leaders. Johanna survived a life-threatening medical injury but lost her sight at age thirteen. It changed everything. Johanna was forced to relearn the activities of daily living in an entirely new context beginning with moving about a room without assistance, dressing herself, and eating a meal. Johanna's first adjustment to blindness was to learn to travel independently in the now foreign environments of her home, school, and community.

Independent travelers are aware of their position in space and relationship to the environment. Johanna learned caning skills by interpreting the variations of "tap, tap, tap" and sweeping her cane broadly across her body to locate any impending barriers. Using a cane requires her to "see" in another way.

Johanna memorized routes and learned how to cross streets in controlled (lighted) and uncontrolled intersections. One time she fell down thirteen cement steps because she misjudged the location of the steps and just stepped off into space, crashing down the stairs. Traveling requires trial-and-error learning, faith, resilience, courage, and protective gear.

Johanna dresses in the dark. She uses a system for putting things away in order; this allows her to locate them later. She distinguishes the front of her clothes from back with safety pins secured to the back label and avoids pattern clash by purchasing clothes in solid colors. She keeps her tennis shoes permanently tied to save time and slips them on like a well-worn pair of bedroom slippers. All clothes are washed on the same cycle (permanent press and warm water) to reduce the dangers of mixing colors or ruining her clothes with too much or too little action or too much or too little heat. This requires an understanding of systems, compromise, creativity, and a sense of humor.

Eating is a challenge for the visually impaired. Johanna locates food on her plate by clock position—meat at 6:00, potatoes at 3:00, salad in a bowl at 9:00 next to the plate, and so on. Johanna avoids rice in restaurants because it is too hard to find on the plate. She believes that pizza is nature's gift to the blind—you get a full meal in a box with beverages on the side! Johanna cooks food in the microwave by pressing the one-minute key and listening to the bell to count the number of cooking minutes, and later she retrieves her food with the sound of another bell. She fries her hamburgers on the stove and avoids the oven—some things are just too dangerous without assistance. It takes planning, innovation, sometimes avoidance, and a willingness to clean up a mess.

Even though she could not read Braille with her fingers (due to damaged nerve endings), Johanna learned the Braille code as a language because it allows her to access talking and voice-recognition technology. She uses a tape player at warp speed, sailing through spoken text like a graduate of a speed-reading program. Johanna dials the phone with her tongue and has a respectable phone bill that competes with the best of compulsive phone-a-holics! Learning a language and using technology require diligence, hard work, overcoming fear, and learning.

Johanna talks to people at the right time by figuring out when to speak or listen in the flow of conversation. It is difficult and confusing to participate in conversations without visual clues. Does the pause in conversation mean the speaker is finished, or did the speaker pause for dramatic effect? Still, she is genuinely interested in others and takes extra time to reach out to others, knowing that her disability is a barrier to some.

Johanna forms an opinion about people by what she hears, not by what she sees. Everyone looks fine to her. She listens with acceptance and remembers the smallest details about others. Effective communication and building relationships require acceptance, openness, patience, intelligence, intuition, and caring.

There's more to this true and inspiring story, but you have probably already figured out my point—all of these experiences prepared Johanna, my beloved daughter, for leadership. She has many of the qualities and abilities that leaders need to contribute and serve others. Here's a brief list:

- "Seeing" in another way
- Traveling around obstacles
- Trial-and-error learning
- Faith
- Resilience
- Courage
- Understanding systems
- Compromise
- Creativity
- Sense of humor
- Learning languages and using technology
- Diligence
- Hard work

- Overcoming fear
- Becoming a cultural interpreter
- Figuring out when it is okay to talk
- Being genuinely interested in others
- Reaching out to others
- Listening
- Acceptance
- Openness
- Patience
- Intelligence
- Intuition
- Caring

The qualities and abilities of leaders are a factor of your success when they are linked to the situation requiring leadership. For example, when are acceptance and caring factors in leadership? When do persistence, innovation, and adaptability serve us well? When is total honesty, as evidenced by complete and timely disclosure, the best course of action? Think of the qualities that are needed by leaders in your organization right now—do they have the right stuff? Do you?

We learn some of the lessons of leadership from our experience, and the rest we learn from others. The loss of Johanna's sight was what some may describe as a "growth provoking opportunity." This was true for Johanna and her family. Adversity is a tough and demanding teacher and builds character. We have little choice except to learn. The experiences of struggle and survival shape your developmental journey in life and become part of the "real" you.

Johanna is a leader in my life and inspires me. Take a moment to think about the people who are leaders in your life. Why are they important to you? What qualities do you wish to emulate? How did they become leaders of your life? What does this mean for your development as a leader? Once you identify these qualities, think about how you would describe them and how these qualities can contribute to your effectiveness as a leader. Here are a few examples of a leader's qualities:

- *Effective leaders are wise.* They see and know what is real in most situations and make good judgments—better than others might make with the same information and opportunity. The source of the leader's wisdom is insight, knowledge, experience, and intelligence. Wise leaders take risks and learn from their success and failures. They know when and how they can have the most productive effect on many situations requiring leadership. Wise leaders know who they are, what they know, and the limits of their knowledge and experience.

- *Effective leaders are learners.* Passionate about learning, these leaders are curious and self-directed learners. They are voracious readers and enhance their knowledge for their personal and professional development. The source of the leader's learning is knowledge of the field, experimentation, experience, study, and accomplishment. Developers of people, leaders as learners embrace organizational learning as a priority and see their role as a learning coach and guide.
- *Effective leaders are accountable.* Accountable leaders are aware of their values and intentions and willingly hold up their behavior and performance to the scrutiny of others. Leaders who are accountable recognize the importance of goal accomplishment and the costs associated it. They are willing to be judged on both the process and the results of their work. Leaders who are accountable ask for feedback, reflect on what happened, and learn.

The examples above illustrate some of the qualities that are highly valued in leaders and reflected in their actions. What are the qualities that define your leadership? How do your qualities explain some of your opportunities to lead or your ability to consistently gain the support and trust of others?

LEADERSHIP CREDIBILITY—YOUR INTENTIONS AND ACTIONS

Your leadership identity is similar to your personal identity—it is made up of your unique qualities, values, beliefs, actions, and experiences as an individual and leader. You reveal your leadership identity to others with your actions. Credible leaders are consistent in their words and actions. They do what they say they are going to do. Credibility is believability. You earn credibility by living the qualities and values that are the hallmarks of your leadership in your daily life. If there is a credibility gap, the base of support for your leadership rapidly evaporates.

Credibility is the match between word and action—doing what you say you will do (DWYSYWD).[7] The actions in your personal and professional life must be consistent with your values. *People listen to your actions, not your words.* During times of great change and crisis, credibility grows in importance due to the uncertainty of the external environment.

Leaders also represent the credibility of the organization. "To earn and strengthen leadership credibility, leaders must do what *we* say *we* will do—DWYSYWD." (do what you say you will do).[8] Leaders, representing the larger vision and commitment of the membership, must establish credibility in their personal and professional lives and in the life of the organization or community they represent. The call for ethical leadership is a call for credibility in words and actions tied to the moral standards or values of the members and community.

The credibility-building process is (1) achieving clarity of a shared vision, values, or purpose, (2) building unity around a common cause or purpose, and (3) ensuring intensity where the effort, purpose, and action are consistent.[9] The loss of credibility produces a reputational crisis that predictably results in the decline of leadership capacity and influence. When credibility breaks down, nothing else that leaders do matters.

There are many valued qualities associated with leaders and leadership. Perhaps the most defining qualities of leadership involve the legacy we leave behind. Did you make a positive difference while leading and participating in acts of leadership? Were productive results achieved? Was your leadership valuable? Your performance as a leader is based on the degree to which (1) the potential of people and the organization is developed, and (2) the long-term success of the organization is ensured. Some measures of leadership effectiveness are not evident during the yearly performance-review process but are reflected over time.

THE STANDARDS TO MEASURE YOUR SUCCESS

Your experience in social groups shapes the development of your adult expectations and standards for leadership, contribution, and service. At an early age you learn about the rights and responsibilities of group membership, including information about roles and relationships, what is important, and how to get along with people. During the adolescent years, social or cultural conditioning is examined in a new light. Some expectations are discarded while others are adopted, refined, and reincorporated into our adult lives.

Your internal standards consist of those cultural understandings that you embrace as a result of a conscious choice, as well as those that are unexamined and unalterable as a result of social conditioning. The difference between values that are freely chosen and those that are unquestioned is informed action—you are operating from either choice or conditioning. These factors are part of understanding what leadership is about and the "right way" to lead. This is worth thinking about. What is the source of your ideas about leadership?

The external standards for leadership are derived from a "socially constructed" view of leadership in a general sense (how the culture defines leaders and what we expect of them) and professional ideals. Over time these ideas can also become part of our personal or internal standards. Organizations need a representation of themselves, and leaders may symbolically represent the "ideal" employee or community member.

Your view of effective leadership is shaped by the requirements of a specific field and role (e.g., national government and president, or education and superintendent). An example of a cultural expectation is that all leaders must have excellent "people" skills, while an example of a professional expectation is that principals should be instructional leaders focused on increasing student achievement. Managers in corporate settings should help employees achieve higher levels of productivity and adopt innovations to increase efficiency and effectiveness. Religious leaders should inspire us and lead exemplary lives. Athletic leaders should serve as role models for youth and exemplify teamwork and sportsmanship in their actions. Government leaders should serve us and avoid "politics." The key word here is "should"! What expectations in your current field or role can you own? What is troubling? How do these cultural and professional expectations relate to your internal standards?

David Maister describes the term *professional* in a different way: "Professional is not a label you give yourself—it's a description you hope others will apply to you. You do the best you can as a matter of self-respect."[10] He describes professionals as those who serve, are committed to serving, and the like—back to the qualities of leadership! Banks McDowell describes the internal dimension of a professional as acquiring "the *character* of a professional," which has two components: (1) "to master and practice the expertise of the profession to the highest level of competence the individual can manage," and (2) "to use these high levels of competence to serve others."[11]

Expectations, ideals, and standards are dominant factors in the way that we think about and measure our success. They serve as a basis for decisions, explain our responses to leadership challenges, and become the yardsticks by which we measure our success. Leaders must balance their internal standard for leadership with the external standards of excellence that are imposed by others and professional practice.

The internal standard is clearly what is most important to you as a result of your social conditioning and experience. The external standards reflect your view regarding what is expected and how others will judge your actions. We end up internalizing many of the cultural standards in our professions and communities. When the internal and external standards are congruent, there is less conflict and more opportunity for support from others when tough decisions are required.

The most difficult decisions are those that challenge these standards. This challenge gets at the core of your identity. It causes great distress and puts you at risk of psychological stress and isolation. The choice to deviate from one's standards can have serious consequences for individuals and leaders. Leaders who try to lead in ways that are not natural or consistent with their values, qualities, and motivations for leading do so with great turmoil and crisis. Many become disillusioned when their reason for leading and working with others is in opposition to the role expectations in a group and threatens their career and livelihood. Consider the inner turmoil of the "whistle blower," who has a conflict between doing what is right based on personal ethics and doing what is expected based on what others view as the "right" course of action. Whistle blowers risk rejection and threats to their survival; it is an act of courage to break the code of silence and resist the pressure to conform to the group.

Consider the classic example of becoming a "company man." The company man, as portrayed in literature and film, sacrifices personal identity and values for the bureaucratic values of the organization. This results in the loss of self and leads to alienation in the work environment. Leaders who abandon their core values to comply with unethical practices are in crisis. They have subordinated themselves to others or the situation and are no longer leading. Developing an awareness of your standards for leadership as influential factors in your actions is critical to your success as a leader.

Your standards help you respond to the question, why am I here and what am I supposed to do with my life? Mature leaders lead an "examined life," where action and reflection are central components. Central features of leadership are action and contemplation. Parker J. Palmer's *The Active Life: A Spirituality of Work, Creativity, and Caring* describes action as an expression of ourselves and states, "Through action we both express and learn something of who we are and the kind of world we have or want."[12]

Contemplation is "*any way that we can unveil the illusions that masquerade as reality and reveal the reality behind the masks.*"[13] The leader's inner life and purposes do matter. These influence the way he or she defines and frames leadership in various situations and whether or not his or her actions are driven by choice or compulsion. What is the state of your inner life? What motivates you to lead? How credible are you? What standards define your success? What capacities do you bring to leadership? How can you increase your ability to contribute and serve? These are the questions of leaders and leadership.

DO LEADERS MAKE A DIFFERENCE?

The easiest way to answer this question is to try to identify examples and nonexamples of situations when leaders made a difference. It is possible to think of situations where leadership made little or no difference, some difference, or was a significant influence on the outcome of a situation or condition. It is also possible to think of some negative examples of leadership that appeared to stop all progress and even cause us to regress! Take a moment to mentally compose a list of leaders who had a positive effect on others.

Your list of these leaders would probably come from all walks of life and include politicians, revolutionaries, ministers, public servants, heads of corporations, citizens, and more. Perhaps we should ask a different question: to what degree do leaders make a difference, and what was the outcome of their efforts—positive, negative, or some of both? Here's a strategy you might use to make this determination:

1. Select a specific situation and examine the full context in which leadership occurred.
2. Step back from the immediate situation and learn about the group life and history of this event; examine the short- and long-term effects of change and the future.
3. Define leadership—what is leadership in this situation?
4. List all the potential factors that influenced the results, including the actions of leaders and members.
5. Rank the factors using the best available information, in terms of their relative influence on the outcome.
6. Establish a standard regarding how much any factor, including the "leader" factor, must affect change in human groups to "make a difference"—10 percent, 50 percent, or more? What about the other factors or elements?
7. Assign each factor a percentage representing its importance in the outcome.
8. Be prepared to explain and defend your decision to others based on the facts and your analysis (be well prepared—others may not agree with you!).

The above process applies the Elements of Leadership and is a tool to assess the effects of leader actions on situations and events. Although this is not an exact tool, it can help you gauge the impact of a leader on various situations. You can learn about how some leaders are able to have a greater impact on a situation by examining the events and figuring out the effects of their actions. One powerful source of learning is the success and failure of others.

The most important question for your development is, How can and when do leaders make a positive difference? You can't control many of the Elements of Leadership, but you can work on yourself! *The potential for leaders to make a positive difference is ever present.* What matters is your development as a leader and your potential to make a difference.

Some leaders do make a difference. They often make the greatest difference during times of chaos and change.

Leaders may articulate the collective will and actions of the membership and serve as agents of change. Their actions can result in peace. Some leaders transform communities. Sometimes leaders change the world by a single act of protest or a lifetime of imprisonment to free the spirit or bring about radical change. Does it take extraordinary effort or circumstances for leaders to matter, or can the daily actions of leaders make a real difference in the way we change and grow? What is the impact of leaders on the process and acts of leadership? How can you develop the leader within you to be more likely to contribute and serve others?

Perhaps some of the factors that may explain how leaders make a positive difference include the standards they set for themselves and others, what they accomplish, and what they learn from the experience of belonging, serving, leading, and learning. Leaders appraise their performance through a process of data gathering (getting feedback on *what* was accomplished and *how* it was accomplished), introspection, reflection, and change. These are the leader's tools to assess and evaluate the impact of his or her leadership and to compare his or her performance with both internal and external standards for leadership.

The leader is only one of the five elements of leadership, and the degree to which leaders can influence the process or outcome of leadership depends on the leader in conjunction with the other four elements. Effective leaders appreciate their capacity, develop their potential, stay true to their intentions and actions, and work with others to achieve the common good. Leaders initially serve as members and gain their authority to lead from the rights and obligations of group membership. Effective leaders serve the membership and understand the role of members as critical participants in leadership, the subject of the next chapter.

NOTES

1. Russ S. Moxley, *Leadership and Spirit: Breathing New Vitality and Energy into Individuals and Organizations* (San Francisco: Jossey-Bass, 2000), 168.

2. See George M. Prince, *The Practice of Creativity* (New York: Collier Books, 1970), for a description of leaders as guides in the creative process. Practical strategies for conducting meetings to facilitate problem solving are described.

3. Burt Nanus, *Visionary Leadership: Creating a Compelling Sense of Direction for Your Organization* (San Francisco: Jossey-Bass, 1992), 8.

4. Nanus, *Visionary Leadership*, 16–17.

5. Ronald A. Heifetz and Marty Linsky, *Leadership on the Line: Staying Alive through the Dangers of Leading* (Boston: Harvard Business School Press, 2002), 73.

6. Bernard Bass, *Bass & Stogdill's Handbook of Leadership: Theory, Research, and Managerial Applications,* 3rd ed. (New York: The Free Press, 1990), 563.

7. James M. Kouzes and Barry Z. Posner, *Credibility: How Leaders Gain and Lose It, Why People Demand It* (San Francisco, Jossey-Bass, 1993), 47.

8. Kouzes and Posner, *Credibility*, 47.

9. Kouzes and Posner, *Credibility*, 48–49.

10. David M. Maister, *True Professionalism: The Courage to Care about Your People, Your Clients and Your Career* (New York: Touchstone, 1997), 19.

11. Banks McDowell, *Ethical Conduct and the Professional's Dilemma* (New York: Quorum Books, 1991), 17.

12. Parker J. Palmer, *The Active Life: A Spirituality of Work, Creativity, and Caring* (San Francisco: Jossey-Bass, 1990), 17.

13. Palmer, *Active Life*, 17.

CHAPTER 3

Members

How did we come to see followership as the antithesis of leadership rather than followers as collaborators in the effort of organizational work?

Robert Kelley, 1992

WHO IS REALLY LEADING?

Leadership is a group strategy and a collective action between leaders and members. It is not a byproduct of a single individual's actions. A common myth is the idea that leadership is embodied in the efforts of a single individual who is the central actor and agent of change. Based on this idea of leadership, the only thing that is needed for a more promising future is "better leaders." But leaders can't lead without followers, and many followers are also leaders. *Leadership is not about what leaders do, but rather about what leaders and members do together when they take action.* We are all leaders and participants in leadership.

The view of leadership as an effect of a single individual's actions limits our opportunities and fails to take into account what we know about the participation and contributions of "members" (often referred to as followers). *A "leader" is any member who consistently acts on behalf of and for the benefit of others. A "member" is any individual who belongs to a group and participates in acts of leadership.* Leaders and members identify problems, create solutions, participate in decisions and actions, and accomplish results.

The term *follower* implies that the leader has the right knowledge and provides direction and strategy to less capable followers. This is not consistent with the reality of any successful effort—it takes many people to lead and participate. The roles of leaders and members are often blurred and shared. The term *member* implies an active and legitimate participation in the process of leadership. The term *member* replaces the term *follower* in *The Elements of Leadership* as a clearer (and more respectful) representation of what really happens when leadership occurs.

Followers have an 80 to 90 percent influence on the results, while leaders account for only 10 to 20 percent of the results achieved.[1] When the success of a major accomplishment is attributed primarily to the superhuman qualities of leaders, the contributions of followers are diminished. This is called the "high cost of leader worship."[2] You might ask, "Who is really leading?" In some situations, the positional leader takes charge, while in other situations, leadership emerges from the membership and is shared.

Max De Pree, author of *Leadership Is an Art*, describes the importance of emergent leaders or "roving leaders" and the need to share leadership:

> Roving leadership is the expression of the ability of hierarchical leaders to permit others to share ownership of problems—in effect, to take possession of a situation. When roving leadership is practiced, it makes demands on each of us—whether we are a hierarchical leader, a roving leader, or a good follower. It's a demanding process. It demands that we be enablers of each other.[3]

Roving leadership exists in environments where leaders are accessible and genuinely interested in fostering participation. There are a variety of factors that influence whether people will support leaders through acts of participation. The work itself must be meaningful to people. The leader's motivation to serve is another factor that influences participation. But fundamental to participation is the relationship between leaders and members. Participatory leaders establish "covenantal relationships" with people that foster risk, sharing, intimacy, and freedom.[4] De Pree describes the purposes that participation serves:

We would like a work process and relationships that meet our personal needs for belonging, for contributing, for meaningful work, for the opportunity to make a commitment, for the opportunity to grow and be at least reasonably in control of our destinies. Finally we'd like someone to say "Thank you!"[5]

Many leaders are motivated by a desire to make a difference in the lives of other people. What is your motivation? Some leaders are more effective than others in certain circumstances and gain the support of others over time. Why do you think some leaders sustain the support of members or colleagues, while others lose their support rather quickly? Effective leaders recognize their own limitations, capitalize on the talents of others, and acknowledge the power and contributions of individuals and the group. Effective leaders understand that the members are authentic participants in leadership.

SHARING LEADERSHIP

When leadership is shared, leaders and members frequently trade places, sometimes leading and sometimes following. When leadership is shared, power is shared. The authority to direct, decide, and act and the responsibility for doing so flow between and among the members and leaders as a result of inclusive processes. The collective intelligence of the group is brought to bear on locating opportunities and addressing challenges. Solutions flow to the center of the process from anywhere in the system.

The best ideas surface as a result of a culture of inclusiveness and creativity, not from a hierarchy that emphasizes power "over" others rather than power "with" others. Although role distinctions and the real or inferred threat of coercive power always exist, leadership and empowerment seek to reduce the impact on this power differential on the creative pursuit of the general good. This is absolutely critical to the survival of groups, organizations, and communities during times of chaos when the answers to perplexing situations are not easily known. In addition, the notion that authority comes from position is rejected by most as a legitimate source of power. There are too many examples of the abuse of power to allow it to exist unchecked in our lives and institutions.

When there is routine work, the established roles and operating rules of the system take care of most things. When the route to the future is filled with complexities, uncertainties, and the unknown, nothing short of a new idea of leadership is needed. Just as leaders must redefine their role, so must "followers," or members, of an organization. We no longer have the luxury of choosing to participate or passing the blame for ineffectiveness on to leaders—we share the solution and the blame for what happens.

Leaders have the responsibility for rethinking their roles and transforming the role of follower to that of member. Robert E. Kelley summarizes the complementary roles of the leader and the follower:

> In reality, followership and leadership are two separate concepts, two separate roles. They are complementary, not competitive, paths to organizational contribution. Neither role corners the market on brains, motivation, talent, or action. Either role can result in an award-winning performance or a flop. The greatest successes require that people in both roles turn in top-rate performances. We must have great leaders and great followers.[6]

MEMBERS AND MEMBERSHIP

I selected the term *member* in *The Elements of Leadership* to challenge the stereotypical view of followers as passive and mindless drones. In contrast to "followers," members are active, intelligent, and contributing participants in leadership. Just as there are effective and ineffective leaders, there are also passive and contributing followers. Kelley identified four types of followers: (1) alienated, (2) passive, (3) conformist, and (4) exemplary.[7]

According to Kelley, the characteristics that distinguish different types of followers are (1) the ability to think critically or uncritically, and (2) active or passive participation. Exemplary followers think critically (independently). Exemplary followers choose to actively participate instead of using their critical thinking skills to protest and undermine leadership and withdraw from participation (alienated followers). Passive and conforming followers think uncritically, but differ in their willingness to actively participate. Conformers are willing to do the work, but don't ask them to think![8]

What factors contribute to the likelihood that members are active participants and critical thinkers? The participation of the members in acts of leadership includes but is not limited to the following:

1. The individual's or group's prior experience with leaders or supervisory personnel (what happened the last time the individual or group asked for help?)
2. The opportunity to genuinely participate and influence what happens
3. The effects of organizational culture on individual and team work (does the system reward competition, collaboration, or both? What is valued?)
4. The opportunity to genuinely participate and influence what happens
5. The degree to which the work is meaningful and supportive of an individual's or group's mission and goals
6. The opportunity to genuinely participate and influence what happens
7. The absence or presence of a threat to the survival of the organization
8. The opportunity to genuinely participate and influence what happens
9. The opportunity to become involved in meaningful and challenging work
10. The opportunity to genuinely participate and influence what happens
11. The opportunity to develop one's talents and learn
12. The opportunity to genuinely participate and influence what happens
13. And more

My friend Alison Page, vice president of safety at Fairview Corporate, Inc., said to me, "People don't leave organizations, they leave bad supervisors!" Leaders have a direct impact on the participation of the members in acts of leadership. Every interaction between a coworker, supervisor, or subordinate is an opportunity for building trust or breaking it down. Relationships between leaders/managers and employees must be founded on the idea of the genuine involvement and participation of others.

WHAT IS CHEESE?

In *Who Moved My Cheese?* Spencer Johnson[9] describes the difficulty people have dealing with change with a simple story. There are four mice, and they each respond to change in a different way. The moral of the story is that change is hard and when your cheese moves, you need to move too! I have been thinking about a different book title. What if the book were called *What Is Cheese?* Cheese can represent anything that you want that is valuable to you and is rapidly disappearing.

As individuals, we define our cheese in different ways. My cheese is the opportunity for meaningful work, making a difference, flexibility, creativity, working with creative and courageous adults, reading, learning, and interacting with colleagues in an academic environment. What is your cheese? When was the last time someone asked you what you want to do and what you enjoy doing? This is an important question for leaders to ask of everyone around them. What motivates one person may be quite different from that which motivates another employee.

I had a conversation once with an administrator who believed that I would find a committee assignment exciting. My first thought was, how little she knows me! I am capable of doing many different things, but I want to do creative work. I can work through an issue in a highly charged and contentious political environment; I just don't like it. Effective leaders get to know people and figure out how to set them free. They intentionally look for opportunities to match people's potential and desires with opportunities. They rescue them from work that drains them, and when that's not possible, they distribute it fairly.

ORGANIZATIONAL DESIGN

Management structures in organizations reflect a range of approaches to leadership. A highly structural and autocratic approach to leadership concentrates the power at the top and reserves many decisions for top-level management. Responsibilities and roles are defined with precision, and the members have limited access to power. This approach promotes predictable and uniform processes for the accomplishment of work.

At the other end of the continuum is participatory leadership, which promotes the design of more "open" or flat organizations, where power is more widely distributed among the members. Layers of management are eliminated, and more power and authority are concentrated in work teams. Structural control is relinquished in favor of greater empowerment accomplished through interdependent work units.

There are obvious benefits in either strategy. Highly structured work settings can produce predictable results and eliminate the wasted human energy needed to constantly examine and define routine work or processes. A controlled and hierarchical structure with explicitly defined tasks can increase productivity, but it can also limit opportunities to increase productivity by blocking opportunities for innovation and change.

An open or organic approach to organizational design promotes continuous "restructuring" of roles and tasks, flattening of the management structure, and using teamwork to provide for greater creativity and flexibility. This approach allows for more individual and team ownership and control over the work and pushes decision making to the "shop floor." The risk in this model is the lack of structure in roles or tasks, which may cause wasted energy and resources, inconsistent results, or both. There are fewer people monitoring the work and ensuring that results are obtained.

How should people work together? What is the most favorable organizational design? The answer is—it depends! Often highly structured organizations find a way to develop programs that increase employee participation, while flattened organizations depend on cross-functional teams and networks to solve the "structural" problems inherent in the work. Structure, task definition, and roles are functions of the group and are best understood in terms of the purposes and needs of the membership.

Leadership and Power

Real differences in power, authority, responsibility, status, and privilege between leaders and members must be acknowledged. These forms of power can be described as personal and positional.[10] Personal power comes from expertise and relationships, while positional power comes from the ability to reward and punish or the legitimate power of a position. According to Bass, "All sources of power yield influence. In real-life situations, leaders draw consciously or unconsciously on multiple sources of power."[11]

The leader with positional power controls resources and the decision-making process. What the leader does with the "power cards" sets the stage for the participation of members in the activities of leadership. If the leader uses the power cards to coerce, the members comply, withdraw, or sometimes overthrow their leaders. If the leader uses the power cards to initiate participation and the genuine sharing of knowledge, the members are more likely to engage in productive work and accomplish the goals that are adopted.

Followers or members have power as well. Think about what might be written on the "power cards" of members. You might see items such as failure to comply, avoidance of assigned work, refusal to volunteer for extra assignments, slowing down in the work, and missed deadlines or "sick-outs" (calling in sick to protest). Sharing power is the only way to avoid the toxic conflicts that take place when "power over" is the dominant mode of management.

Participation and Collaboration

What characterizes genuine participation of the members and the ability to influence what happens? Involving people in the goal-setting process acts as a motivational factor in their performance.[12] The benefit of collaboration is not just in goal setting, but also in the exchange of knowledge. Once a goal is established and people believe it can be achieved (collective self-efficacy), the process of goal attainment becomes a motivational factor more powerful than the members' involvement in the goal-setting process.[13] The belief that one can accomplish the goal (perceived self- and group efficacy) and the exchange of knowledge through collaboration are two significant factors that affect performance and the attainment of goals.

Shared decision making is accomplished through the organizing structure of group work and "process facilitation." *Process facilitation is a communicative strategy for tapping the collective knowledge of the group and directing this knowledge to solve novel and intractable problems and plan the future.* The leader convenes the group to learn, create, and take action.

The facilitator's toolkit is filled with strategies to help people to examine their thinking and break the constraints of the limiting assumptions that lie beneath the surface of our thought. Facilitation is both a process and an attitude about the value of participation and engagement. As a process, it involves organizing people in a variety of group settings to accomplish work. As an attitude, it requires us to identify the assumptions or mental models that block us from thinking creatively and dynamically about relationships, culture, and the redesign of work.

Our attitudes about situations and solutions are represented by what Peter Senge calls our mental models. According to Senge, exposing our mental models allows us to discard them and adopt new ones:

> The practice of working with "mental models" helps us to see the metaphorical pane of glass we look through and helps us re-form the glass by creating new mental models that serve us better. Two types of skills are central to this practice: reflection (slowing down our thinking process to become more aware of how we form our mental models) and inquiry (holding conversations where we openly share views and develop knowledge about each other's assumptions.[14]

Sharing assumptions and a spirit of inquiry set the stage for learning and the discovery of knowledge. Since the goal of group process is generally aimed at strategic action, the end result of the process is a decision. Genuine participation is evident when information is widely shared, the level of participation is appropriate to the importance of the decision, the underlying causes, issues, and assumptions are identified, and the members' contribution to the final decision is visible. The greater the impact of the decision on individuals and the organization, the higher the level of member participation required.

A core leader and member skill is knowledge of effective group dynamics. In formal settings, the group leader facilitates processes to encourage critical and creative thinking, problem finding, and futuring. In informal settings, teams work together to solve the routine and non-routine challenges of their family, work, or community lives. Process facilitation does not always require a facilitator, because members in "leaderless groups" are empowered to take charge of themselves and work in teams to determine a collective strategy for change.

Beware of the danger of inauthentic processes overshadowing real collaboration and teamwork. My friend and colleague Dr. Bob Brown commented one day on inauthentic processes. He referred to them as "process without a point!" Process is inauthentic when the decision gets made elsewhere, the decision doesn't matter, or there was no decision to make in the first place. Our participation doesn't really matter, and we know it. This has the effect of breaking trust, discouraging participation, and alienating even the most dedicated and idealistic members.

There are benefits and hazards to group processes. The benefit of group process is obvious: when it works, $1 + 1 > 2$. Collective thinking in most cases is superior to the thoughts of any single individual, particularly when problem analysis is complex and the solutions involve multiple and interdependent functions. On the other hand, the threat of "groupthink" is real:

> *Groupthink* is the collective striving for unanimity that overrides group members' motivation to realistically appraise alternative courses of action and thereby leads to (a) a deterioration of mental efficiency, reality testing, and moral judgment and (b) the ignoring of external information inconsistent with the favored alternative course of action.[15]

When groupthink occurs, the group selects the decision that avoids risk or controversy as a way to preserve the group rather than address the problem. Even in "leaderless" groups, there are differing amounts of power and influence, and the members who belong and participate in relationships have differing affective and social needs. These are factors of group processes and influence the outcome of group work.

The exclusion of diverse voices and ideas in both individualistic and harmonious cultures thwarts meaningful group participation. The individual voice is silenced in cultures valuing harmony, when it invites conflict, even productive conflict, or threatens the survival of the group. The individual voice is not shared in cultures valuing competition because individuals withhold their good ideas to improve their own position, often at the expense of the group.

Another danger of group process is that it can limit the creativity of individuals. The leader's role is also to preserve the balance between "I-ness" and "We-ness" in the organization—knowing that creativity resides in individuals and groups. Although this appears contradictory, the work of pioneers and pioneering teams must coexist to better ensure the survival of groups, organizations, and communities.

LEADERSHIP AS A GIFT

The opportunity to lead is a temporary gift bestowed by the members, and it can be revoked at any time. Leadership is not something that is "done" to others, but rather an exchange of value and a gift of service. Members make the decision to participate with leaders when the cause is just, the direction is sound, the strategy that is proposed is likely to be successful, and there is confidence regarding your potential or experience as a leader. Leaders create opportunities for others to lead through delegation, participation, engagement, and support. Leadership as a social exchange also rewards leaders and members alike with money, recognition, or continued employment. But leadership can also be a transformational experience, where members achieve more than one would normally predict because of the relationship that is established between leaders and members. Bernard Bass and Bruce Avolio describe three leadership models: (1) transactional operator, (2) team player, and (3) the transformational, "self-defining" leader.[16] Each leadership model has a different idea of followership. Leaders and followers exchange work and value for their own benefit in the transactional model. The leader gives the follower what he or she needs in exchange for getting what the leader wants. The team player model emphasizes the leader's need for acceptance. The leader gives followers respect in exchange for being affirmed and liked. Finally, the transformational model is based on the idea of the leader supporting worker autonomy to accomplish organizational goals. This requires the leader to "be concerned about values, ethics, standards, and long-term goals," incorporating followers as authentic participants.[17]

Leaders have a relationship with the members. Members, as active and intelligent participants in leadership, are willing to act when they are provided input, are engaged in the process of decision making, and have some control over their lives and choices. Employees continuously assess the leader's work and their willingness to participate. Authentic participation is evident when members collaborate with each other and share leadership.

Leaders and members have a reciprocal relationship, and the responsibility for the relationship and achievement of goals is mutual. Leaders who take action without involving others soon find that they are unable to motivate or influence people to support their direction. Members who push the responsibility for decision making and participation to leadership are instruments of their own powerlessness.

The saying "that's what you get the big bucks for" promotes the idea that the leader is the only one responsible for success or failure, getting credit or taking the blame, not the membership. Acts of coercion (threats of punishment or withholding of rewards) produce defiance in the membership. A strike is the most symbolic and visible symbol of the members' refusal to participate. Strikes occur when the actions of leaders are considered unjust.

It is impossible to define the role of leader without acknowledging the interaction of the leader with the members of the organization and the context or situation that requires action. To be successful, leaders must be good members and create the conditions that develop the potential of others for leadership. There is an implicit risk in any leadership act—you are putting your ideas and yourself out there and asking for support. If your ideas are sound and results are achieved, you will increase your leadership opportunities by earning the respect of the membership.

Leaders must continuously ask for and earn the support of members and are only leading in the larger sense when they regularly offer something valuable to others that is accepted and produces a positive result. It is an exercise of leadership to give power and authority to others and establish a climate where participation, dialogue, and inclusiveness are real and valued.

What factors contribute to the likelihood that others will support your leadership? These factors include but are not limited to the following:

1. Your personal and professional track record
2. Your willingness to share leadership
3. Your knowledge and expertise in some situations
4. Your willingness to share leadership
5. Your ability to frame a problem that makes sense to others
6. Your willingness to share leadership
7. Your ability to begin an initiative or get others to address a problem
8. Your willingness to share leadership
9. The way you treat others
10. Your willingness to share leadership
11. Your relationships with individuals and groups
12. Your willingness to share leadership
13. Your ability to facilitate a process that leads to a solution
14. Your willingness to share leadership
15. And more

These and other factors impact your ability and opportunity to influence and work with others toward a desired goal or direction. Leaders influence the process and the results. Effective leaders work successfully with people, create opportunities for others to lead, and provide for the long-term stability of the organization. They focus on how the people of an organization should work together to achieve its goals. Leaders inspire commitment by creating organizations that unleash the capacity, creativity, and leadership of others. *The leader's work is the work of the membership.* In the next chapter, the challenge of the "situation" and its effects on leaders and members are described.

NOTES

1. Robert E. Kelley, *The Power of Followership: How to Create Leaders People Want* (New York: Bantam Doubleday Dell Publishing, 1992), 20.
2. Kelley, *Power of Followership,* 19.
3. Max De Pree, *Leadership Is an Art* (New York: Dell Publishing, 1989), 49.
4. De Pree, *Leadership,* 60.
5. De Pree, *Leadership,* 23.

6. Kelley, *Power of Followership*, 41.

7. Kelley, *Power of Followership*, 97.

8. Kelley, *Power of Followership*, 97.

9. Johnson, Spencer. *Who Moved My Cheese? An Amazing Way to Deal with Change in Your Work and in Your Life* (New York: Putnam, 1998).

10. Bernard Bass, *Bass & Stogdill's Handbook of Leadership: Theory, Research, and Managerial Applications*, 3rd ed. (New York: The Free Press, 1990), 250.

11. Bass, *Bass & Stogdill's Handbook of Leadership*, 250.

12. Albert Bandura, *Self-Efficacy: The Exercise of Control* (New York: W. H. Freeman & Company, 1997), 462.

13. Bandura, *Self-Efficacy*, 462.

14. Peter M. Senge et al., *Schools That Learn: A Fifth Discipline Fieldbook for Educators, Parents, and Everyone Who Cares about Education* (New York: Doubleday Dell Publishing Group, 2000), 68.

15. David W. Johnson and Frank P. Johnson, *Joining Together: Group Theory and Group Skills* (Boston: Allyn and Bacon, 2000), 302.

16. Bernard M. Bass and Bruce J. Avolio, *Improving Organizational Effectiveness through Transformational Leadership* (Thousand Oaks, Calif.: Sage Publications, 1994), 14–20.

17. Bass and Avolio, *Improving Organizational Effectiveness*, 19.

CHAPTER 4

Versatility and the "Situation"

A stretch of freeway just twenty-five miles south of Long Beach, California, was the site of one of the biggest car crashes in freeway history. On November 3, 2002, forty-one people were injured and 194 vehicles were damaged as a result of a chain-reaction pileup of cars, closing a busy freeway for eleven hours. Amazingly, no one died at the scene.

The largest single factor that caused the pileup of cars was the fog. The visibility was down to fifty feet when the crashes began just before 7:00 A.M. on a Sunday morning. The other factor named as a cause of the multiple accidents was human error; drivers failed to reduce their speed to a level consistent with the road hazard created by the fog.

None of this was surprising to me (except the magnitude of the crash) until I watched a news segment about the research conducted by the National Transportation Safety Board (NTSB) on factors associated with foggy conditions and driver behavior. NTSB studies of accidents show that some people actually drive faster when they experience fog![1] Apparently, the condition of fog changes the perspective of drivers who would normally slow down if they were aware of the impending danger. The fog reduces their perspective and causes people to lose track of their speed. They charge ahead because they can't see what's there that would cause their driving behavior to change. Suddenly, they find themselves participants in a multiple-car crash that catches them unprepared to stop and fighting for their lives.

The experience of leadership can cause a multiple-car pileup unless you have a perspective on what it's about and how you fit into the scene as a leader and driver of change. You are more likely to be successful if you fully understand the situation and you know what types of actions or "leader behaviors" are a match with it. Many would say that "situational knowledge" is not all there is to leadership, but providing the right kind of leadership at the right time is an asset to leadership.

Some leaders are "in a fog" because they don't understand what is going on around them and continue to work with others in the same way, regardless of what is occurring. This generally causes people to shake their heads and wonder about how this person got his job and why he thinks that anyone would follow him. One way to think about getting perspective is to imagine yourself on the dance floor and simultaneously standing on a balcony looking down on yourself and your partner and the rest of the dance floor.[2] Leaders must step outside of the action and see the bigger picture and gain perspective and the long view. This is true while you are actively leading and after your service is over.

Perspective allows you to frame your experience within a larger context and helps you to understand the dynamics of the situation and your role. It puts you in touch with what might be needed and what you can realistically offer to others. Versatile leaders are sensitive to the unique requirements of the situation and adjust what they do and how they work with others accordingly. They also recognize that some situations make a critical difference while others do not demand their involvement or commitment. What does it mean to be a versatile leader?

VERSATILE LEADERS

Versatile leaders initiate and orchestrate processes to address problems or locate opportunities by uncovering the unique requirements of situations and capitalizing on the talents and collective knowledge of the membership to identify strategies and take action. *The "situation" refers to the unique characteristics and task requirements of any novel situation where acts of leadership and participation are needed to solve problems, take advantage of opportunities, or both.* Situational factors include, among others, (1) the nature, context and complexity of the situation, (2) the knowledge and experience of leaders/members regarding how the situation is understood and may be solved, (3) the expectations of leaders/members of each other under certain circumstances, and (4) the range of opportunity regarding how a situation can be managed.

Since leaders and members vary in their knowledge and experience in any novel situation, this is a collaborative exercise. If the situational demands are well known and previously encountered, it is likely that processes and procedures are already in place to address the situation. Anyone who knows how the problem was solved previously can lead—this includes supervisors, team leaders, or peers.

When the situation is not known and the environment is highly unstable, more leadership and collaboration are required. No one holds the key to all the knowledge needed in each situation. Many situations are highly complex, requiring us to examine problems beyond the immediate situation to identify the underlying issues that are not readily apparent. It takes high levels of expertise to understand complex problems and opportunities and to identify the most viable course of action.

Often members possess the knowledge that is needed to solve problems in many situations. The practical intelligence or expertise of seasoned or veteran employees is highly valuable. "Practical" intelligence is nonacademic knowledge gained from experience. Experts have special skills in problem definition and solution: they (1) draw from their extensive knowledge and see larger patterns in problem analysis, (2) conceptualize problems in a more sophisticated way and spend more time defining problems, and (3) have a higher level of awareness regarding the complexity of problems and the impact of potential solutions on the final result.[3]

The situational knowledge of experts is extensive and has a significant impact on any situation. In cases where the leader is also the expert, there is likely to be a high level of respect from members, and people expect the leader to use his or her expertise to provide direction and solve problems. However, many thorny problems require the collaboration of many experts from different disciplines to understand the complexity of the problem in a way that leads to an effective decision. A quick directive from the leader may be highly effective or counterproductive to the satisfactory resolution of the situation. It depends on the leader, the demands of the situation, the level of expertise needed to understand what's going on, and the level of ownership required once a course of action is decided. This is a complicated formula and requires a sophisticated approach to leadership.

Some situations are new to our experience, while others have some common characteristics and patterns that are known. For example, many school leaders have experienced a bomb threat and know the basic steps of crisis management. Although this knowledge does not diminish the seriousness of the threat, leaders can respond with some confidence, working with emergency-management personnel to reduce the threat to safety and manage the crisis until stability is restored. There are some "situational challenges of leadership" that can be anticipated, and you can benefit from the experience of others. Some examples of these situational challenges are transition, crisis, change, and the future.

Seasoned leaders have a large repertoire of strategies, which allows them to respond flexibly to a variety of situations. They are comfortable with leading and sharing leadership and are sensitive to the changing needs of people and the organization. They have versatility because they can adjust and vary their behaviors based on the situation and needs of the members or followers. This is an important aspect of leadership in various situations.

YOUR LEADERSHIP STYLE

Your leadership style consists of your preferred ways of leading and interacting with others. You might think of your leadership style as a constellation of some of the more enduring qualities, characteristics, beliefs, and behaviors that define the authentic you and your relationships with others. Your personal development, life experience, talents, and education have shaped your leadership style. Some of the most common elements that define your leadership style are as follows:

- Interactions with people (social or interpersonal style)
- Methods for accomplishing goals (including your priorities and work habits)
- Methods of processing information (cognitive style)

• Highly valued and frequently demonstrated leader behaviors and actions that you have found to be generally useful in many different situations (your previous leadership experience and accomplishments)

Your leadership style is developed from trial-and-error learning, imitation, education, and experience. When others allow you to lead often enough, you build a track record of success and a recognizable style. This style is evident when people are generally aware of how you will work with them as a result of their previous experience. When people experience your leadership, they quickly learn how you may be helpful to them in certain circumstances. It is easy to determine whether someone's actions and decisions are helpful. If positive results were achieved and the process was professional, your success will be acknowledged. This information is stored by your colleagues, supervisors, subordinates, or all three, and retrieved when the next situation arises.

When you lead in your preferred style and that style fits the situation and the needs of others, you can respond to challenging situations with great insight and skill. Your leadership style is reinforced every time results are achieved, positive feedback is received, or more opportunities to lead are provided to you.

Leaders, like experts in any field, build and refine their knowledge and skills and become sensitive to the context and the situational demands of each challenge. If you enjoy getting to the task immediately and minimizing the small talk, you may prefer to work with others by focusing on tasks and efficiency. If you enjoy socializing and making sure that everyone is comfortable, you may prefer to focus on building a team and promoting collaboration to achieve goals. Sometimes people with a very technical orientation find themselves short of people skills when they are promoted to manager, principal, or division head. Suddenly a very successful employee can find himself or herself in a very uncomfortable role.

The duties of managers, principals, directors, or corporate leaders involve working with people. You may be someone who values relationships and struggles with establishing a realistic schedule to complete projects. Building relationships is a very valuable asset in many work settings. It can also be a cause for concern if your people orientation results in a lack of structure and uncompleted work.

If you like to see the detail, you may soon recognize that you need help from someone else to see the big picture. If you like to direct others because of your need to exert influence or control, you may discover that this takes power away from others and sooner or later they end up doing less and you end up doing more. Your role as a leader is to be an astute observer regarding the demands of any situation and the characteristics and maturity of the people you are working with at each decision point. A general rule of thumb is to develop the leadership capacity of others by empowering them through support and decision-making opportunities.

Even though you can't fundamentally change who you are, you can continue to develop your capacity to lead and modify your behavior to meet the needs of people and the requirements of a situation. Successful people strike a balance between their drive to accomplish and their desire for acceptance and building relationships with other people. Balancing the achievement of goals with the needs of people is one of the challenges of leadership.

The key to your success is understanding your preferred leadership style/behavior and knowing the circumstances or conditions under which your style matches the needs of members and the situation. You can learn when to change for the benefit of others. Successful leaders are highly aware of their style and how to modify it. They avoid responding routinely to every situation, using the same pattern of responses despite the needs of followers or the situation.

When you "overextend" your style by applying it to every situation, you can quickly become a nonleader and even a roadblock to the success of others. Some leaders fail to provide what is needed because they have not developed themselves fully, have failed to recognize their own limitations, or haven't learned how to encourage the leadership of others. This lack of flexibility or versatility in their leadership style causes many ups and downs in their performance and creates a vacuum in leadership that is soon filled with dissension and uneven results. When leaders are able to provide what is needed *most of the time*, they earn the respect and support of others and add value to the organization over the long run.

Your leadership style can be either effective or counterproductive in any given situation. Some leadership styles have limited effectiveness in most circumstances. For example, coercive leaders are bound to fail because coercion produces defiance and subversion. You aren't a leader if your style diminishes the performance of others or limits the capacity of the organization to change and grow. Coercion produces revolutions, not results.

Some situations are highly complex and require a combination of styles at varying times to meet the needs of followers and the situation. The more complex the situation, the more versatility in leadership style is needed. Your leadership or the leadership of others can emerge to fit any situation if you are humble and flexible enough to accept it from others and share leadership.

As a leader, you may need to explain a process or interpret data. Sometimes you need analytical and creative thinking skills to figure out a problem. Leaders need the ability to build relationships and communicate effectively with others. As a leader you must figure out what is needed and share leadership. You can't do it all. There are times when you may clearly possess what is needed and what you have to give others is of real value. There are other times when your limitations interfere with your success and need to be managed. Effective leaders are highly self-aware and know their strengths and limitations.

THE STRENGTHS AND LIMITATIONS OF STYLES

If you were to make a list of the things that you do well, what would be on your list? Are you great at achieving goals? Are you innovative and comfortable with change? Does the idea of meeting new people and building a team inspire you? Do you know how to organize things and make things run smoothly? Are you an effective communicator and skilled at motivating people to work toward a higher goal? Your strengths are the key to your success. These are the things that have contributed to your success and are valued by others. When your strengths match what is needed, you are working in your preferred style. You instinctively know what to do, and you are good at it.

Some leaders have a preferred style that is so dominating that it becomes a liability or a danger to them, not a strength. Your strength becomes a liability when you routinely offer the same approaches to every situation, despite the needs of people or the requirements of the situation. When this happens, you are "overextending" your leadership style and relying too heavily on a limited range of approaches.

Versatile leaders recognize that what is needed in any given situation may not be what they prefer to do as leaders, requiring them to leave their comfort zone and stretch to meet the needs of others and the situation. A description of eight leadership styles or themes follows. Notice the strengths of each theme or style and also the dangers when the style is overextended and becomes a liability. Your preferred style is made up of how you participate in work and what you think leaders should do as a primary strategy for working with others. Are you an achiever, team leader, systems leader, relater, innovator, coalition builder, inspirational leader, or developer? Try to locate at least two of these styles that are a match with your personal leadership style.

Achiever[4]

Achievers base their success on getting results. They are goal-oriented and provide structure and energy to the accomplishment of tasks. They are highly productive and are known for their ability to get things done. They are often recognized for their expertise.

Strengths

- Focus on the achievement of goals by establishing a climate of accountability and measuring goal accomplishment
- Model the standard of work expected; take responsibility for getting the work done
- Make sure that tasks are clarified and connect the efforts of individuals to the goals of the organization
- Set an example by being one of the most knowledgeable and diligent workers in the organization

- Focus the effort of people on achieving the goals; frequently ask, how does this effort relate to the goals we have established?
- Develop action plans and schedules; keep track of the progress of individuals, departments, and the organization's attainment of goals

Dangers

- Fail to delegate because they want to get the job done quickly and correctly
- Postpone celebrations and relaxation until everything is done and ignore the social needs of people
- Create unrealistic expectations related to workloads and timelines
- Act too fast to fix problems or take on too much work (ensuring that other people do less)
- Burn out employees because the cost to their personal and professional lives is too high

Coalition Builder

Coalition builders form strategic alliances to enhance the power and resources of the organization. They build a network of key communicators and organizations and continually work to gain and keep their support. Their desire is to understand politics and use a political strategy to achieve results.

Strengths

- Persuade others by understanding the needs of individuals and groups and connecting the satisfaction of these needs to the goals of the organization
- Know people and understand the roles and relationships between and among individuals and departments; use this knowledge to get actions supported and problems resolved
- Identify key players and determine ways to meet their needs through negotiation and collaboration

- Keep up with the internal and external politics; create coalitions of various stakeholders to get things done
- Identify constituents and build ownership for the organization's direction by securing everyone's vote with an "election style" campaign
- Scan the environment to detect changes and adapt; anticipate the impact of change on the stability of the organization

Dangers

- Negotiate for the wrong thing, sometimes developing a political position instead of recognizing that a moral decision is needed
- Align themselves with the "old guard" and fail to connect with new people and groups—becoming elitist
- Make too many deals and use deal making as a strategy to solve problems that are not political (e.g., issues of professional practice)
- Fail to use participative processes and lose touch with what's going on inside their organization or in the external environment

Developer

Developers place their confidence and trust in the ability of people to be self-directed and autonomous learners. They provide opportunities for individuals and teams to learn through systematic professional development. Developers focus on reflective practice and support action research as a primary tool to implement and evaluate reform.

Strengths

- Express confidence and trust in the ability of people and encourage them to take charge of their own personal and professional growth
- Work with people to help them discover their interests and talents; help people identify goals for their individual growth and development

- Coach individuals and teams based on their developmental stage; focus on the needs of individuals and provide the appropriate level of assistance
- Frequently ask, What are you good at? Where do you want to go? How can you take responsibility for your own growth? When can we begin?
- Value life-long learning and promote individual, team, and organizational learning
- Believe that the key to organizational success is learning and reflective practice
- Participate in professional development activities and believe that learning is critical at all stages of life

Dangers

- Fail to hold people accountable for their learning; learning is not applied to improve work practices
- Support too many programs so that learning is not leveraged for overall system improvement
- Rely solely on professional development to solve issues of poor employee performance (some employees can't get better)
- Rely too heavily on learning as the only strategy for improvement and ignore other opportunities (data analysis, restructuring, etc.)
- Fail to connect professional growth activities with measures of individual, department, and organizational growth
- Believe that the solution to every problem is another class!

Innovator

Innovators identify the winning idea that, if selected, will bring about the greatest opportunity for growth. Innovators support pioneers, encourage risk taking, and initiate pilot efforts. They assess the readiness of people for change and monitor the adjustment of people during a change effort. They are risk takers and bring energy and enthusiasm to new initiatives.

Strengths

- Understand the challenge and processes of change
- Select and support initiatives that provide for broad participation
- Motivate and inspire people to takes risks
- Know the critical role of pioneers and identify people with unique talents and support their development and autonomy
- Support innovation by creating flexible work groups, sponsoring pilot projects, adopting many approaches, and creating a culture that values and rewards innovation
- Protect the organization from a diffused effort with too many change initiatives and monitor the "pot" to make sure it does not boil over and derail the initiative

Dangers

- Adopt too many reforms and create too many layers of change, resulting in no change at all
- Cause employee burnout and system fatigue due to poorly timed and poorly implemented change efforts
- Fail to listen to the constructive analysis of proposed change efforts (sometimes no change is the right answer)
- Push to innovate without sufficient planning
- Fail to revise their ideas when the change effort is ill advised or ineffective (falling in love with the change itself)

Inspirational Leader

Inspirational leaders create organizations that are driven by operating principles and employ democratic values. They create excitement, energy, and enthusiasm around inspiring ideas. They inspire others by minimizing the distinction between leader and follower and ensuring that the values of the organization are consistent with policy and practices.

Strengths

- Persuade people to enroll in their vision and direction by creating excitement, energy, and enthusiasm around inspiring ideas

- Employ democratic values to define how people are to work together and treat each other
- Provide support where it is needed at any level of the organization to remove the artificial distinctions between leader and follower— everyone's work is honorable and valued
- Build the "character" of their organization by connecting a core set of beliefs to decisions and directions
- Tell stories to articulate the core beliefs and values; beliefs are consistent with daily interactions and decisions
- Build a strong culture and celebrate the contributions of people and the success of the organization
- Ensure that the values of the organization are consistent with policy and practices

Dangers

- Lack good judgment regarding when and how to take an ethical stand (their response is out of proportion to the dilemma)
- Fail to consider diverse, conflicting, and equally important values; fail to recognize that no one has a corner on the truth or on morality in every situation
- Take a dogmatic approach to issues and fail to take sufficient time for ethical reasoning to resolve difficult issues
- Act in ways that are inconsistent with their espoused moral conduct and code, creating a credibility gap

Relater

Relaters have a charismatic ability to connect with people on a personal level and are relationship builders. Interacting with people at all levels of the organization, relaters take the time to listen and talk to people. Relaters build informal networks and rely on people to get the work completed through cooperation.

Strengths

- Build relationships by getting to know people as individuals and make a consistent effort to connect with people on a personal level

- Make personal connections and ensure that people are valued and feel a genuine sense of belonging
- Identify ways for people to participate, interact with others, and build mutual understanding
- Care about people as individuals and employees; use a personal approach and invest the time needed to get to know people as individuals
- Know the names of people, the details of their personal lives, and their history and contribution to the organization
- Develop relationships to accomplish goals by building informal networks in the organization and relying on the goodwill of people to get the work completed through cooperation

Dangers

- Rely on relationships to accomplish too much of the organization's work
- Invest too much time in building one-to-one relationships and miss the opportunity for a team approach
- Show too much "schmooze" and not enough genuine caring
- Use a limited strategy to address significant organizational challenges; assume that if people get along, success is guaranteed
- Consider relationship building as their primary work and avoid responsibility for the operation and results

Systems Leader

Systems leaders view problems as opportunities for group learning and focus on continuous improvement and quality. Systems leaders establish an open system and ensure that involvement cuts across roles and classifications, emphasizing learning through knowledge sharing.

Strengths

- Develop the capacity of people to understand the interaction and interdependence between and among systems; use this knowledge to examine and solve problems

- View problems as opportunities for group learning and system improvement and focus the work of the organization on using system thinking to improve processes
- Support open systems and participation at all levels
- Delegate responsibility to the people closest to solving the problem and empower people to make decisions
- Value integrated approaches and use systems thinking to restructure processes and continuously learn and improve

Dangers

- Use too much process as a substitute for making decisions and taking action
- Risk the subversion of worthwhile initiatives because of "tyranny" of group norms and resistance to change
- Lack sufficient balance between empowerment and decisiveness—committing valuable resources of time and energy to group work
- Use excessive processing of situations as a substitute for judgment and experience during a crisis

Team Leader

Team leaders believe that teams are the primary structure for making decisions and accomplishing tasks at all levels of the organization. Creating flexible organizations and providing time for group decision making, team leaders value the diversity of people and ideas. They insist that everyone's ideas and experiences should become part of any final solution.

Strengths

- Develop teams as the primary structure for collaboration and decision making in the organization
- Create a culture of teamwork, establish achievable goals, monitor the progress of teams, and assist with problem solving and support when it is needed

- Create flat and flexible organizations and give people the opportunity to make decisions
- Value the diversity of people and insist that everyone's ideas and experience are needed to create a successful team
- Involve people in goal setting, problem solving, and improvement activities
- Provide time for group work and make most recommendations after getting input from teams
- Create a structure for teamwork across all levels of work—including the top management structure

Dangers

- Build committees, not teams, and use committees to endorse directions already established
- Fail to establish the parameters for decision making, including the professional standards and practices of the field
- Allow teams to make decisions but do not require teams to take responsibility for teams implementation
- Avoid making decisions and get teams to endorse all decisions as a way of avoiding leadership
- Fail to hear the individual voice and diminish the overall productivity of the organization by placing too much emphasis on teamwork and not respecting and supporting individual contributions enough

The eight styles or themes illustrate that there are many different ways to lead and work with others. Leaders develop their strategic thinking and leadership by understanding when leader behaviors are useful and identifying the strengths and inherent dangers of each approach if it is misused or used excessively. Think about the leaders you know. What style is evident? How has this been a useful style in some situations and dangerous in others? How can you play to the strengths and guard against the dangers of your preferred style?

VERSATILITY

Versatile leaders recognize that each situation may require them to modify their style or even *stretch* their typical or preferred way of working with others to meet the needs of people and the requirements of the situation. Versatile leaders seamlessly draw on their talents and experience in several of their strong areas and match them with the needs of people and their organization. *Versatility as a quality is the ability to move from one thing to another with ease and to readily apply your talents and skills to each new challenge with a fresh approach.* This assumes that you have more than one approach to leadership and that you understand when a particular style or set of "leader behaviors" is most appropriate.

If you have a limited range of responses to people or situations, don't know how to respond to others, or both, then your effectiveness is limited. As you mature in leadership, you grow in versatility (what you can do) and flexibility (allowing others to emerge to lead and serve). Versatile leaders can usually provide effective leadership in many situations but often create opportunities for others to lead to expand the capacity of people and to get more accomplished.

The leader may shift to the role of coach, becoming more flexible in his or her approach to accomplishing goals. Leaders provide support to people who are developing their leadership talents and prepare them for increasingly more responsibility. You don't relinquish your role as leader when you create opportunities for others to lead; you expand your approaches to leadership. People want to work with a flexible leader, and they also want to know what they can usually expect from you when you are leading.

Successful leaders have a "loose-tight" style that allows for flexibility in some circumstances and not in others. It makes sense to delegate some decision making and control to employees while maintaining the rights and responsibilities of management or administration. Leaders are responsible for upholding quality, professionalism, and the standards or expectations of the field.

The following is a story about leader with versatility. This story shows how Ms. M incorporates her personal work style and strengths to provide leadership to others. Sometimes the leadership tasks are easily handled because what is needed is consistent with Ms. M's work and personal style. At other times, Ms. M must stretch to meet the demands of a situation (being versatile) and draw on the talents of others to lead (being flexible). This story illustrates how versatility in approach and style can help leaders meet the needs of people.

MS. M—A TALE OF A VERSATILE LEADER

Ms. M is a vice president of a corporation and is responsible for a large sales division. Ms. M's personal work style is highly focused on accomplishment. Routinely setting goals to stay on task and measure her own performance, Ms. M has a strong personal work ethic. A skilled planner, Ms. M likes to discover the big picture through the details and begins most challenges with solid research. She likes to know the implications of every action before any decision is made or a plan is implemented. Preferring to work independently, Ms. M wants plenty of time to complete a project. Prior to sharing her information with anyone, Ms. M likes to understand the problem fully and identify the alternatives and consequences of every recommendation before consulting with others.

Although Ms. M enjoys social interactions with people, she frequently leaves the office and dines alone at lunchtime to escape work, recharge her batteries, and efficiently accomplish her personal errands. Ms. M says that in her perfect world, "Everyone would understand their jobs, do their best work, get along, and there would be productivity and profit (and a little fun when the work's done)!" Work comes first.

When Ms. M works with others, her leadership style is versatile. She has learned to stretch to meet the needs of her supervisors, colleagues, and subordinates. Some recent challenges demonstrate this versatility. During a strategic planning session, Ms. M was asked to develop a plan to reduce expenses companywide without reducing the number of employees. Ms. M accepted the challenge and worried about how she could solve the problem. She decided to dig in and do her homework for several months.

She studied the operations of the company, analyzed data, considered alternative strategies, and prepared a draft summary of her findings and tentative recommendations. This is a typical work style of an "achieving" leader who sets goals, identifies a thorough and efficient process to complete the project, identifies the standards for success, and proceeds with diligence until an initial plan is formulated.

Even though her ideas are sound and the background and support for the recommendations are complete, Ms. M knows that she needs the support of others to improve the proposal and ultimately carry out her recommendations. After the report is complete, Ms. M systematically and strategically shares a draft of her ideas with colleagues, supervisors, and subordinates, gathering their feedback and ideas. Ms. M "shops" her proposal and continues to refine it until she knows that there is sufficient support for her plan. This leadership style is typical of a "coalition builder" who wins the support of others by identifying potential allies, addressing the concerns of objectors, persuading others through consultation and rational discussion, and winning people over by addressing their needs in the proposal.

Ms. M then holds a staff meeting to enlist the support of the people in her division to implement the changes outlined in her proposal. An "achieving" leader, Ms. M outlines the goals and sets in motion a process to achieve the goals by delegating the tasks and describing her expectations for performance.

Once the goals are defined, Ms. M asks each person how they can contribute to the effort. She listens for new ideas and approaches and encourages creative thinking to generate more alternatives to meet the challenge. The ideas are recorded and posted on a wall for consideration, and people freely share their ideas. Ms. M exhibits the leadership style of an "innovator" who is open to new ideas and establishes a climate where it is safe to consider alternatives.

A second meeting of the strategic-planning group is held and a new employee profit-sharing plan is announced. The leadership group is challenged to promote a change in the way people work together in the corporation. Instead of "making your budget for your department," the new emphasis is on helping each other across the entire company to make the corporate goals and budget targets. If the company goals are met, then there will be profit sharing on an annual basis for every employee. Ms. M calls another meeting. Ms. M knows that this is a major change and develops a strategy to gain the support of employees.

An "inspirational" and "team" leader, Ms. M starts the second meeting by standing in front of the room with a cake full of candles. She asks a few employees to join her to light 120 candles. She tells the employees that the 120 candles represent their total number of years of service to the company. There is plenty of laughter as several people try to light all the candles at once. Going around the room, she calls out people by name and then describes the unique contributions of each person and how they helped to make their division a success. Ms. M shares a chart of the successful sales track record of the team over the last five years to celebrate their success.

As an "inspirational leader," Ms. M knows the value of a good story. She describes how well they have worked together and talks about their first convention and design center. A flexible leader, Ms. M has asked a few employees to make a wall chart of their history as a company and department, and some old photos are shown of the early years. Two of the most productive employees proudly move around the room, standing next to the wall chart and describing what happened. When the presentation is over, the employees applaud.

Ms. M then stands at the podium and says, "If we can do this well without much collaboration across divisions, imagine what might happen if an entire company worked together this way?" The new company profit-sharing plan is then disclosed, and Ms. M takes the time to discuss the financial promise of the change and the opportunities to work together as a team. She passes on her excitement and energy to them and speaks persuasively about the potential benefits of changing from a department or division team to a companywide team.

The rest of the meeting is spent thinking of ways to enhance the sales and service of the other divisions through partnerships. A "systems leader," Ms. M thinks of a way to sell products to customers and eliminate the need for having to receive goods and then ship them out of the warehouse. She explores the idea of an online ordering system that eliminates the warehouse, reduces costs, and allows for better inventory control. She decides to develop a plan to create a catalog-only supply division. Her sales division could make a profit without ever receiving or shipping a single product—a big change in the way they are currently selling their products.

Ms. M thinks about the training that will be needed to increase everyone's ability to work with the Internet as a sales tool. She knows all employees will need to use databases, develop a strategy to establish strong customr relationships that are not based on showroom visits, and learn how to market their products on the Web. As a "developer," Ms. M looks for online courses, individual and group classes, and speakers who can help prepare employees for the change ahead.

She establishes a team to research and plan a schedule of group and individual learning resources related to this new initiative.

The next week Ms. M learns that one of her subordinates has just been diagnosed with a life-threatening illness. As a "relater" who understands how important people are to the organization's success, Ms. M meets with the employee, expresses her concern, and works quickly to assist the employee in obtaining an immediate leave of absence for medical treatment. Speaking to the employee with empathy and encouragement, Ms. M extends reassurance about job security and the employee's future in the organization.

At the end of the week, Ms. M looks over her list of goals and accomplishments. She checks off some items and adds a few more, making sure that she is organized for the next week. A versatile leader, Ms. M knows when she is operating out of her comfort zone or when the situation is a good match with her skills. She writes a few quick thank-you notes to the people who offered leadership to the department this past week. She wants them to know that they are a valuable part of the team and that their leadership is appreciated. Next week the focus will be on developing an action plan and identifying team goals for the new initiative.

Ms. M is a versatile leader because she understands that even though she has individual work responsibilities, her primary role as a leader is to work with people. Leaders provide direct leadership by managing and directing the work of others and indirect leadership by leading through delegation or committee processes. Like Ms. M, versatile leaders are flexible and situational leaders. They are keenly aware of their strengths and limitations.

What is your preferred leadership style? How can you develop your leadership versatility to effectively respond to the needs of members and the situation requiring leadership? How do reflective leaders become more strategic in their approach to leadership? Your preferred leadership style influences your general approach or initial response to the situation, but it should not dominate your response or be a substitute for strategic thinking regarding what approaches or actions may be most valuable in any given situation. Being strategic in your approach is connected to the idea of versatility.

First, you need many approaches to leadership, and then you need to identify what approaches may be useful. Strategic leaders are versatile and flexible. They are dedicated to getting results but not locked into a particular style or solution. An awareness of your strengths and limitations causes a developmental shift in self-knowledge and can result in a new awareness of your role as a leader. After initially focusing on "what I can accomplish" and your leadership style, the mature leader begins to focus on the requirements of a given situation and views people, problems, and opportunities in a larger context. Besides gaining a strategy for leadership, the leader gains an appreciation of what he or she does well. Mature leaders use the knowledge gleaned from the positive and painful experiences of the past to learn and lead more effectively.

Mature leaders shine a light on their actions and performance and identify the reasons for their success, missteps, and failures. This allows them to understand what produces a positive result and what actions may get in the way of their future success. They understand the reasons for and the conditions under which they and others are successful. *Reflection is a self-examination and analysis of your intentions, actions, and results to understand what happened and evaluate the results of action.* Effective leaders examine their actions and performance to increase their understanding by learning how others may view them. They are highly aware of the gap between their real and desired performance, and they learn to become more strategic about their leadership as a result of reflection. You might think of this as a combination of wisdom, experience, and intelligent action.

Even though none of us can change our natural style, sometimes a stretch in style and versatility is needed to give to people and the organization what is needed at any point in time. For example, if a financial loss is anticipated, the leader needs to be tough-minded, determined, and analytical to accomplish budget reductions. On the other hand, during periods of dynamic growth, the leader needs to be a good crisis manager, have excellent people skills, and be willing to take risks.

One way to assess your leadership effectiveness is to find ways to regularly get positive and negative feedback from others about your leadership style and the various approaches that you have used to provide leadership to others. Try to get others to help you assess how well you and the organization are doing and what changes need to be made.

A plan for getting this feedback from trustworthy people is needed to increase your awareness and understanding of your leadership and its impact on others. Ask people to tell you how things are going. Consider your current situation. Look for ways to capitalize on your strengths in your personal or professional life. What additional areas of professional development would enhance your capacity to lead and work with others and increase your versatility?

Effective leaders make adjustments to stretch their leadership style and enlist the support of others to provide the leadership that is needed. They become more strategic in their approach and response to situations. Mature leaders not only understand what they do well; they also think strategically about what people, the situation, or the organization requires at any one point in time. This allows them to be valuable to people and the organization over the long haul. The next chapter describes the impact of groups, organizations, and communities on the acts of leadership.

NOTES

1. See www.ntsb.gov/publictn/H_Acc.htm for examples of reports on safety and car accidents.

2, Ronald Heifetz, *Leadership without Easy Answers* (Cambridge, Mass.: Harvard University Press, 1994), 253.

3. Mark Tennant and Philip Pogson, *Learning and Change in the Adult Years* (San Francisco: Jossey-Bass, 1995), 55–56.

4. See Sarah J. Smith, *Women Administrators: Concepts of Leadership, Power, and Ethics* (Ed.D. dissertation, University of Wyoming, 1996) for the foundational research and development of dominant leader behaviors and themes found in this chapter. A study conducted by the author of twenty-six female administrators resulted in the development of the eight leadership styles described in this chapter.

CHAPTER 5

Groups, Organizations, Communities
—A Survival Story

FIRE WALKING AND OTHER TEAM SPORTS

Would you be willing to walk on a bed of coals ranging in temperature between 1,200 and 1,500 degrees Fahrenheit? Over two million people have participated in fire-walking seminars and walked over hot coals to discover the power of "mind over matter." Fire-walking enthusiasts claim that you can develop your self-confidence enough to walk over the coals through positive thinking and group encouragement. If you visit Tolly Burkan's website (www.firewalking.com), you will discover that the price of this seminar is a mere $10,000.00 for up to 200 people! The seminar promises that the experience changes the way people work together by helping them discover how to conquer both fear and fire with the support of a team.

Although fire walking is a novel idea, the theory behind experiential learning activities is to build individual confidence and group cohesiveness through a "simulated survival experience." The experience of fire walking, surmounting the challenges of an endurance course, or rock climbing places people in situations that require them to trust others and learn together. It demands that participants cast off their usual boundaries, open themselves up to the experience, ask for help, and achieve a mutual goal. Essentially, the goal is to create groups who have faced a challenge and survived. The experience builds trust—at least for the time being!

Why do you think the television program *Survivor* is so popular? If you think about it, it is a simulated survival story. The most difficult challenge the game's "tribal members" face is the need to work together to survive, as well as to compete with one another to win the game. You can figure this out in just one episode (relieving you of the need to watch it again if you hate the program!).

The study of groups, organizations, and communities is in some ways a survival story too. The degree to which individuals are committed to a group is based on how important membership is to their survival, quality of life, or values. Sometimes group membership is a matter of convenience, and our investment is low, or we may not feel a sense of community. The antics that take place "on the island" may be similar to what we observe at work when community is lacking—alliances are formed, people are deceived, self-interest operates more often than interest in the greater good, and so forth!

Effective leaders understand the history and life of groups, organizations, and communities. They know how the group was formed and why it exists, how membership is defined, what happened in the past that explains the present, the potential impact of present actions on the future, and more. The relationship of groups, organizations, and communities to each other is like a set of nested boxes. The smallest unit of a social structure is a group.

Organizations, institutions, and communities are larger structures encompassing many subgroups. For example, the members of a department are a subgroup of a high school. The high school is a subgroup of a school district located in a community that is part of a state and federal system, and so on.

The exchange and impact of group history and life must be located within these various nests and understood using multiple perspectives. The dynamic interaction and impact of many groups, organizations, and communities affect any situation requiring leadership.

FRAME ANALYSIS—SEEING THE WHOLE AND THE PARTS

As an element of leadership, "groups, organizations, and communities" serve as the *backdrop* and *stage* where leadership occurs. As the *backdrop* to any situation, groups have subtle and often powerful influence on our perception and understanding of reality. Knowledge of group history, life, and culture "frames" a situation requiring leadership in an entirely different way.[1] For example, what might appear on the surface as a conflict between two employees may actually be a restaging of conflict between two employee groups that was not resolved during the last round of contract negotiations. Information about group life and history adds detail and context to any situation as part of a larger whole.

The conflict between the two employees just mentioned is about the past and the present. The two employees participate in a culture that shapes their beliefs and values about acceptable ways of expressing conflict (that's the past). The expectation that employees will work collaboratively changes the way that conflict is now viewed in the work environment: conflict must be productive and not interfere with the operation of the team (that's the present).

As the *stage* where leadership takes place, the organization or the community is the setting where leadership occurs, and the leader is a central, but often silent, actor in the drama. For example, two employees might be in conflict at a manufacturing plant with a history of strained labor relations or with a highly diverse workforce. This information screams out at us and changes the potential meaning of the conflict and the roles of the employees. What are the motivation and goals of the actors in this power drama?

There is also a difference between what might be construed as a minor interpersonal conflict between two people and a situation with the potential to cause a strike. Remember Rosa Parks's refusal to give up her bus seat in Montgomery, Alabama? The act of a single individual became the impetus for the struggle against Jim Crow laws. Real change finds us completely unprepared, though often not unaware.

Leaders must understand what is really going on and look at the situation from different perspectives. What if the employee conflict appears to involve two employee groups but is really a long-standing personal feud between two people, and the conflict between employee groups is a fabrication?[2] (A fabrication is a false belief about what is going on.) Multiple views are possible and should be examined in every situation. Leaders need to view situations from many perspectives and use their critical and creative thinking skills to discern and interpret the meaning of any situation.

It seems obvious to say that the size of the stage is important too. Some conflicts take place around the kitchen table, while others take place on the world stage. How much potential does leadership in this situation have to bring about significant change to the organization or community? Back to the employee example, what if your organization has been selected by the union as a symbolic site to protest unfair labor practices? The importance of this element, "groups, organizations, and communities," incorporates all the factors that provide context and help frame a situation so that it can be understood.

Leaders analyze a situation with many different frames to understand it and consider the situation within the larger context of community to interpret its meaning and potential effects. Situations are understood by examining their contexts, relationships, and connectedness to other things, not by analyzing their individual parts or properties. Leaders use systems thinking to make sense of what's going on:

> In the systems approach the properties of the parts can be understood only from the organization of the whole. Accordingly, systems thinking concentrates not on basic building blocks, but on basic principles of organization. Systems thinking is "contextual," which is the opposite of analytical thinking. Analysis means taking something apart in order to understand it; systems thinking means putting it into the context of the larger whole.[3]

Due to our growing knowledge about the interconnectedness of most things, it is not wise to take action without considering any situation within the larger view of networked systems that affect and impact leadership. This helps leaders discover the underlying causes, sources, and meaning of any situation. We are challenged to probe deeper for the underlying issues that are just below the surface, awaiting our discovery.

Lee Bolman and Terrence Deal, authors of *Reframing Organizations: Artistry, Choice, and Leadership*, recommend reframing situations to get a better perspective on any situation. They offer four different frames to interpret the same situation: human resource, structural, political, and symbolic.[4] The structural frame views organizations as structures with defined goals, roles, and relationships. The human-resource frame views organizations as an extended family with individuals needing to fulfill their needs and feel good about getting their jobs done. The symbolic frame views organizations as cultures and the participants as actors on a stage. Organizational life is understood through stories, rituals, heroes, and myths. The political frame views organizations as arenas where people compete for power and resources.

Leaders must understand organizational and group dynamics theory as a "frame" for situational analysis. Leaders use existing frames and develop new frames to understand the parts and the whole as their knowledge expands. "Choosing a frame, or understanding others' perspectives, involves a combination of analysis, intuition, and artistry."[5] Without this knowledge, leaders will fail to detect what is important in any situation. Much of what is important is reflected in the culture of the group or organization.

YOUR ORGANIZATION'S HISTORY AND CULTURE —A SURVIVAL STORY

You might think of the history of any group as a survival story. "Culture is the 'story' of who we think we are."[6] The underlying beliefs and values of an organization are often related to new members as survival stories. Survival stories describe key challenges or opportunities and how these situations or events were successfully resolved. "The legends or stories that constitute myths can be clues to the way a culture views reality—or the way it adapts its beliefs to *fit* reality."[7] James says that these stories become most powerful during times of stress and can interfere with the perception of reality. Stress, crisis, or change can cause us to retreat and cling to our stories, even when they aren't helpful or productive. Stories and myths change based on changes in the culture. Try to think of some myths that are changing in your life and culture.

For example, one myth is that if you are "loyal" to your employer and work hard, then your employer will reward you with job security. This myth is exploding as a result of downsizing, corporate mergers, the burst of the dot-com bubble, and the events of 9-11-01. The reality is that the economy and unforeseen events can have unpredictable effects. We can't know the future, the future is not secure, and job security is a thing of the past. What myths dominate the landscape in your organization? What events or changes are challenging these myths? What stories still deserve to be told?

Jennifer James, author of *Thinking in the Future Tense: Leadership Skills for a New Age*, alerts us to the dangers of cultural or corporate ethnocentrism when leaders "put themselves at the center of the universe and then rewrite history to suit their purposes."[8] She recommends learning the real history of the organization or culture and being alert to how others might perceive this history. The roles and expectations for leaders and members are created and sustained by the culture of groups, organizations, and communities. Leaders shape culture and are shaped by it.

LEADERSHIP AND CULTURE

Culture addresses the important challenges and functions of organizational and community life. Edgar Schein defines group culture as follows:

> A pattern of shared assumptions that the group learned as it solved its problems of external adaptation and internal integration, that has worked well enough to be considered valid and, therefore, to be taught to its new members as the correct way to perceive, think, and feel in relation to those problems.[9]

Schein identifies three levels of culture: artifacts, espoused values, and basic underlying assumptions.[10] Artifacts are what can be seen and interpreted (language, architecture, technology, arts, etc.). Espoused values are those values that are publicly declared as principles or justifications for action. Underlying assumptions are those deeply held values and beliefs that are no longer questioned and are a consistent source for collective action.

Culture affects the ways things are done and how change is supported or thwarted. It is a powerful influence on how leaders and members interact and how participation and involvement are defined and promoted. Understanding, preserving, and shaping culture are core tasks of leadership. Culture can be a life-giving agent providing for both individual and organizational development, growth, renewal, and transformation. It can also be oppressive and diminishing. Leaders and members must become more aware of the underlying assumptions of the culture that sustain and develop the organization and appreciate the risks of maintaining a culture that prohibits growth and change.

Leaders must be detectives of culture and learn as much as possible about culture and its effects. Schein defines some of the critical aspects of culture:

- Behaviors
- Language
- Customs
- Traditions
- Group norms
- Espoused values
- Formal philosophy (ideological principles)
- Rules of the game (the way things are done)
- Climate (the feeling conveyed)
- Embedded skills (special competencies or skills)
- Habits of thinking, mental models, and linguistic paradigms
- Shared meaning
- "Root metaphors" or integrating symbols (emotional and aesthetic responses)[11]

Think of your membership in your family and what you need to understand about your family to be a successful leader and member. This is the same level of knowledge that is needed for leadership. Try thinking of your family's culture and look over Schein's categories of culture. How much do you know about the culture of your family? How much do you know about the culture where you work? Leaders must understand the culture to know what is worth preserving and what needs to be changed because it no longer serves the group well.

People quite naturally resist changes to their culture (after all, this is how the members survived in the past), yet this resistance can also cause the group to decline, and that is unacceptable too. Extreme forms of conformity and rigid boundaries can limit the opportunity for members to grow, change, or participate in other communities. Excessive group compliance becomes a tyranny and works against individual, organizational, or community growth. Thus, the very thing that helped us survive can also threaten our survival—this is the paradox and challenge of group life and change!

When people organize into groups, almost instantly a competitive "we-they" situation is set up in an old paradigm of leadership against those who are not members. This frame operates on the idea that resources are scarce and the best way to maintain one's position is to accumulate resources at the expense of others—competing in an environment of winners and losers.

This competition can produce excessive aggressiveness and work against community. When the group is threatened, we (as members) are threatened too. The actions of members are easily understood when framed in this context. The "tribal members" go to war and eliminate the leaders or conditions that threaten survival! Increasingly, the cost of this kind of "leadership" is too high.

Why is survival such a dominant theme of leadership? The purpose of group membership is the individual and collective development, growth, and survival of its members. Group life provides for many of our human needs. For example, our families and "home" communities are the primary sources of our sense of place, identity, belonging, and development. Our role as employees and members of organizations helps us provide for our families and ourselves and offers the possibility of engaging in meaningful work. Religious institutions help us connect to each other as spiritual companions in search of meaning, God, and the afterlife. We are members of many groups based on our family of origin, ethnicity, geographical region, nationality, religion, or language.

We also define ourselves by our involvement in a profession, lifestyle, economic class, educational attainment or interest, and participation in a corporation, professional association, or club. Groups, organizations, and communities are fundamental to our lives, and as such, they are fiercely protected. Leaders are charged with ensuring the continuity and vitality of the group over time. Leaders facilitate the adaptation of people to their environment. If the group declines or dies, leaders fail.

We measure a leader's effectiveness based on his or her ability to (1) accomplish the goals of the group, (2) maintain or improve the relative position of the group and its resources as compared to other groups, and

(3) ensure the stability and viability of groups, organizations, or communities over time. As authentic group members, leaders must demonstrate fidelity to the group organizational goals and well-being.

Some organizations are loose federations of subgroups, serving as an organizing structure for volunteer activities. Other organizations are tightly controlled entities dedicated to producing wealth. Organizations have unique characteristics, a culture, a process for inducting members, definitions of the rights and obligations of membership, and an expectation that members conform to and remain loyal to the group.

Because community is global and the actions of smaller communities impact the whole, the strategies for leadership and survival are changing. Former competitors now collaborate, and mergers of interests and markets increase efficiency and effectiveness. A new view of leadership, group and organizational life, membership, citizenship, and community is emerging.

DIVERSITY, INCLUSION, AND COMMUNITY

The most basic idea about diversity, inclusion, and community is summarized by this simple question, how can we be different together?[12] Breaking this question apart, reveals two more questions: (1) how are we different? and (2) what does it mean to be together? We are different due to our multiple cultural identities. But locating a cultural identity is complicated. My friend Tullio Maranháo was a citizen of the world. He was born and raised in Brazil and was a United States citizen. He was a tenured full professor at the University of St. Thomas in St. Paul, Minnesota. He taught as a visiting professor in Germany, Canada, and France. He spoke five languages and understood more. When he died, his memorial service was mostly in English and partially in Portuguese. What was his cultural identity? How do you define your cultural identity?

The explosion of diversity in twenty-first-century life has dramatically altered the face of our society and the amount of cultural knowledge needed in daily living. The history of this explosion can be traced to the post–Cold War period in many countries in the world and to the Civil Rights movement. When the "wet blanket" of political oppression caused by the Cold War was lifted, it produced a political struggle for (1) individual human rights, (2) cultural human diversity, and (3) global human opportunities.[13] These "Good Things" were getting in the way of each other, and collisions caused conflict all over the world. Harlan Cleveland described the social revolution of the twentieth century as "the outbreak of diversity—the boiling over of resentments in the name of almost forgotten or newly discovered cultural traditions."[14]

We are increasingly more culturally complex, and so the idea of belonging to a cultural group may be yet another myth of society. Leaders are community builders who honor differences with a spirit of inclusiveness and community. Basically inclusiveness means that everyone belongs. Our differences add value and complexity and are a gift of human life.

One of the barriers to community is the "cultural baggage" that we carry in our own suitcases, including our familial, national, and even corporate values.[15] The values that are promoted are often those of the dominant group, creating a feeling of exclusion and a climate of misunderstanding. Instead, multicultural organizations and communities need to create new cultural understanding by first recognizing and learning about differences and then appreciating how these differences add value and contribute to the flexibility and adaptability of the community as a whole.

Leaders need to make room for and appreciate differences to promote inclusion in their own lives by experiencing many cultures and participating in them. They need to take the time to ask people how they define their cultural identity instead of operating on preconceived notions or assumptions.

The commitment to becoming culturally adept is evidence of respect for and inclusion of others as authentic participants in our lives. Sarah Lawrence-Lightfoot defines "the six windows of respect—empowerment, healing, dialogue, curiosity, self-respect, and attention." [16] Empowerment is recognizing that people need to take charge of their own lives. Healing shows respect through the ethic of care. Curiosity and attention refer to the qualities that are needed to build and honor relationships. Self-respect enables us to preserve our own dignity and support the dignity of others. Dialogue is the give-and-take of mutual interaction, combining heart and mind.

"IF I SEE IT, THEN IT'S THERE"

During the final stages of preparing a statewide document in the late 1980s, a small group of people reviewed it and the recommendations in the report. The report described educational opportunities for students. The goal of the report was to define and expand the idea of students with high potential and to develop policies that would be more fully inclusive of *all* students, particularly students of color. The language of the document referred to "*all* students" and made no specific mention of under-represented populations including students of color, students with disabilities, or students who were not native English speakers. I had placed the word "all" in italics to draw attention to the idea that "all" meant everyone. I struggled with the text. If I listed some groups, but not all groups, would that contribute to the exclusion?

Mae Gaskins, the assistant commissioner of education at the Minnesota State Department of Education during this time, read the document. She raised her concern that students of color were not specifically mentioned in the report. I shared my concern about listing some cultures and not being able to list them all. Gaskins understood and replied that sometimes it is important to list a certain group by name, just to make it visible. She said, "If I see it, then it's there." I understood immediately her point—sometimes you have to see something to know it's there. Sometimes you have to see it and say it loudly and clearly, like the statements below:

1. There are too few people of color in leadership roles, and it is a serious problem for all of us.
2. White males benefit from their privileged status and have more opportunities to lead.
3. Women who aspire to leadership need more credentials and experience to get promoted, and even when they get the job, it is made more difficult by the conflict over gender-role expectations and leadership.
4. For many people inclusion means being allowed to participate without being aggressively promoted to leadership roles.
5. There is an inherent suspicion that people of color or women are not qualified to lead and that it is a risk to give them power. The

risk is that the culture and rules will change. And yes, that will (and should) happen.

6. We need more leadership from everyone and specifically from those who have the "gift of marginality" because of their race, sexual preference, religion, gender, disability, or any other factor.[17]

Individuals and organizations should actively engage in developing people for leadership, particularly those from populations that have been historically underrepresented. We develop our cultural awareness and understanding of each other through dialogue.

DIALOGUE

Leaders must understand the nature of dialogue and be skilled in this conversational form as a method of promoting acceptance, learning, and cultural understanding. Dialogue is a conversational form of "sustained collective inquiry into everyday experience and what we take for granted" and involves a three-stage process:

> First comes *surfacing assumptions:* making yourself aware of your own assumptions before you raise them. Second comes the *display of assumptions:* unfolding your assumptions so that you and others can see them. The third component is *inquiry:* inviting others to see new dimensions in what you are thinking and saying, and to do the same for the assumptions of others.[18]

This definition of dialogue requires us to deliberately unfreeze our assumptions or mental models, gain new perspectives (that later become assumptions), and create new knowledge. We must suspend for awhile what is known and what is assumed so that a new perspective is discovered that was not imagined before the conversation began. This purpose of dialogue—to reach a decision, achieve consensus, or locate the truth—is called the teleological view of dialogue.[19] Dialogue is a communicative process that is characterized by discovery, respect, and commitment:

> Dialogue is guided by a spirit of discovery, so that the typical tone of dialogue is explorative and interrogative. It involves a commitment to the

process of communicative exchange itself, a willingness to "see things through" to some meaningful understandings or agreements among the participants. Furthermore it manifests an attitude of reciprocity among the participants: an interest, respect and concern that they share for one another, even in the face of disagreements.[20]

Dialogue can occur even when neither party knows where the dialogue is headed or whether the outcome will result in a common view. The goal of the dialogue is to understand in "the gesture of turning to the Other with goodwill."[21] During the process of dialogue, roles are suspended, and the dialogue between equals produces new learning and understanding, even when diverse and contradictory views are present and not reconcilable. Dr. Maranháo, a colleague and friend, shared the following personal story with me in September 2001:

Dr. Tullio Maranháo owned a beach house. The neighbors hired a security guard to protect their homes from theft and vandalism. One day Maranháo talked to one of the guards, and they became friends. After many conversations, Maranháo learned about the guard's "second job." When the guard was off duty, he would go to another city, join a gang of kidnappers, kidnap a wealthy person, and demand money for the hostages.

Maranháo related that he seemed like a "good guy," and he was shocked to learn of this other "occupation." He decided to keep talking to the guard, even though he knew that it was dangerous. Maranháo, an ethicist and anthropologist, decided to learn what he could about the guard's life and his experience.

One day the guard asked Maranháo for help with a question: was it wrong for him to use the gun provided by the association in the kidnappings? This question startled Maranháo and caused him to ask more questions. How did the guard view his situation from a moral perspective? He wondered why the guard seemed concerned with the ethics of using the gun and not concerned about the kidnapping. A conversation ensued.

The guard shared his ethical principles: It was important that none of these crimes took place in his community. He was dedicated to his commitment never to injure people or to jeopardize the property in the neighborhood he guarded—this was his job! Kidnapping "corrupt" businessmen allowed him to provide for the safety and future of his family. It was an exchange of value, their lives for money. His employment as a security guard was insufficient to support his family, but honorable work. He viewed both jobs as the only response to his living conditions.

What is the lesson of leadership in the story of the security guard? Maranháo went on to describe the importance of viewing the situation by suspending judgment. He described the *violence* of intense poverty on people, the corruptness of the system and those who profit from it, and the desperate living conditions of people and their response to it. The lack of morality in society regarding access to wealth led the guard to act in ways that work against humanity.

Maranháo told this story to illustrate the idea that *it is possible to understand another's view without reconciling it with our own beliefs*. What would lead us to participate in acts to save our families or respond to inhumane conditions? Maranháo advanced the realistic possibility that in a postmodern world, we might merely be able to expect to understand or know another's thoughts, not necessarily to agree with them.

The process of dialogue opens us up to change and greater understanding of the human condition. The purpose of dialogue in this context is *the process itself, rather than the outcome*. Dialogue does not exist when the conversation is a replication and repetition of power relationships played out in debate, but rather when "the language of dialogue consists in the acceptance of dissent."[22] Maranháo pushes our thinking by challenging us to open up to the experience of others for understanding and change.

We cannot avoid our cultural imprints, prejudices, or life experience as we enter dialogue. But the ideal of dialogue requires that we block out the noise of our background, experience, and the lens of cultural judgment (to the degree possible) and that we listen and understand. How can dialogue inform and expand leadership and develop communities? The challenge of leadership is to suspend the underlying assumptions and see what is below the surface of group, organizational, and community life.

According to Laurent A. Park Daloz and others, leaders must develop "certain habits of the mind that steady them in turbulent times and foster humane, intelligent, and constructive responses," including the following:

- The habit of *dialogue* (meaning through interaction)
- The habit of *interpersonal perspective taking* (seeing through the eyes of the Other and responding with empathy)
- The habit of *critical, systemic thought* (seeing parts and connections as patterns)
- The habit of *dialectical thought* (working with contradictions and reframing one's thoughts)
- The habit of *holistic thought* (seeing life as an interconnected whole leading to *practical wisdom*)[23]

When the dialogue is authentic and the ideal is achieved, the speaker and the listener are changed by the encounter. The spirit of dialogue builds community. Dialogue allows us to see what is there and to acknowledge the barriers to community. A significant barrier to community is the difference in power, access, and opportunity that is a result of our membership in various groups.

LEADERSHIP AND POWER

Group affiliation can be either a source of power and privilege or a source of oppression and disadvantage for people based on their role, status, and membership in various groups. Power, status, position, wealth, control, and opportunity vary based on a person's relative position, role, or group membership. The obvious differences in power, resources, and access prevalent in communities are mirrored in groups and organizations. There is always a "ruling class." Peter Block, author of *Stewardship: Choosing Service over Self-Interest*, describes the ruling class of managers and executives:

> It is only a bit of an overstatement to say that the ruling class in our culture is our managers and executives. They are the class of people who drive much of what we do. They control the majority of our resources; they are the heroes of the American dream. We have no royalty, no powerful church. It is the executives of our organizations who pave our streets with gold.[24]

"Elites," those belonging to highly advantaged groups, are leaders and the beneficiaries of leadership. Leaders have a high-status role in organizational and community life with plenty of power and access to resources. Those who are disadvantaged find themselves in "follower" roles with limited opportunities to move up in position or status. This creates an inherent adversarial relationship between management and labor. Robert Terry shares a parable about "the ups versus the downs":

> What makes an up an up and a down a down? An up can do more to a down than a down can do to an up. That's what keeps an up up and a down down. Ups tend to talk to each other and study the downs, asking the down's what's up, or what's coming down, for that matter.[25]

The parable of the ups and downs illustrates what we all know is true: that there are real differences in power between and among people and that this has a large effect on most everything. Terry goes on to describe his hope and disappointment at the lack of learning that occurs whenever a down becomes an up:

> I used to think that when downs became ups they would carry over their insight from their downness to their upness. Not so. Smart down, dumb up! One can be smart one minute, dumb the next.[26]

Social class is a form of personal and group power and determines whether one is an up or a down. When leaders preserve the social order and more wealth is created for already advantaged groups, this makes leaders and organizations (in some sense) corrupt because they continue the domination by advantaged groups. The exception is when the group's goal is to reform the system. But even in reform groups working outside the system, the issues of power and control are problematic. Power, access, the distribution of wealth, and opportunity are central problems of human life.

LEADERSHIP AND DEMOCRACY

If leadership is a moral activity, then how does one reconcile the goal of ensuring the "common good" with the possibility and reality of the oppression and exclusion of some? This question is obviously too large for this slim volume. However, there is at least one obvious response: Leaders are obligated to build cultures that develop potential and move us toward freedom, justice, and community. If there is to be an advantage to membership, it should be on the basis of contribution and participation, not unequal access to power and influence. This is a core value of democracy.

Leaders can address issues such as access, opportunity, justice, and inclusion by changing the culture, policies, and structure of organizations. Some of these efforts involve recruiting, hiring, and mentoring members of disadvantaged groups into leadership roles, providing opportunities for greater interaction and participation between and among diverse employees, examining and changing employee compensation that appears unduly influenced by class, race, or gender, and more. Leaders have a responsibility to improve organizations and communities by refusing to participate in overt or covert acts of bias and privilege and by engaging in community-building activities.

Peter Block addresses this moral responsibility by advocating stewardship, defined as "the willingness to be accountable for the well-being of the larger organization by operating in service, rather than in control, of those around us. Stated simply, it is accountability without control or compliance."[27] He advocates choosing service over self-interest. Block challenges leaders to change the balance of power and eliminate dominance, promote a more equitable distribution of wealth, and eliminate the paternalistic practices that promote dependency rather than empowerment.

Leaders must acknowledge the real differences in power and access that exist between and among employees and groups in the internal and external environment and commit themselves to making their organizations and their communities more humane.

The pursuit of justice, freedom, and community is closely linked to cultural understanding, inclusion, and an appreciation of differences. Dialogue, a tool to facilitate cultural understanding, is a process for uncovering our assumptions, sharing our experiences, and discussing the undiscussable.

COMMUNITY

The definition of community is changing. Historically, communities consisted of people who lived or worked near each other or people who shared similar ideologies or backgrounds and were geographically close to one another. This allowed people during an earlier time to participate "in some kind of a commons—a shared, pubic space of the sort that anchored the American vision of democracy."[28] However, today location and proximity may not be factors in defining a community. The concept of community has become global in nature and scope.[29]

The existence of "virtual" communities, consisting of people connected through technology, is evidence of the emerging global nature of community. The "new commons is global in scope, diverse in character, and dauntingly complex," requiring us to think about citizenship in an entirely new way.[30] We now understand that the actions of people inside their own "communities" affect us all. This makes it impossible to take action without considering the effects of leadership on a larger scale.

Leaders are charged with the responsibility of ensuring the survival of groups, organizations, and communities. The responsibility for leadership and change rests with all of us. Harlan Cleveland says, "No individual can be truly 'in general charge' of anything interesting or important. That means everyone involved is partly in charge. How big a part each participant plays will much depend on how responsible he or she feels for the general outcome of the collective effort."[31]

We have an individual and collective stake in leadership as members of human communities. Only leaders and members together, sharing membership in many groups, organizations, and communities, can change themselves and their communities. The impact of change and the future is described in the next chapter.

NOTES

1. See Erving Goffman, *Frame Analysis: An Essay on the Organization of Experience* (New York: Harper & Row Publishers, 1974), for a discussion of "frames" and their use in interpreting experience.

2. Goffman, *Frame Analysis*, 83.

3. Fritjof Capra, *The Web of Life: A New Scientific Understanding of Living Systems* (New York: Bantam Doubleday Dell Publishing Group, 1996), 29–30.

4. Lee Bolman and Terrence Deal, *Reframing Organizations: Artistry, Choice, and Leadership*, 2nd ed. (San Francisco: Jossey-Bass, 1997), 15.

5. Bolman and Deal, *Reframing Organizations*, 270.

6. Jennifer James, *Thinking in the Future Tense: Leadership Skills for a New Age* (New York, Simon & Schuster, 1996), 22.

7. James, *Thinking*, 75.

8. James, *Thinking*, 42.

9. Edgar H. Schein, *Organizational Culture and Leadership*, 2nd ed. (San Francisco: Jossey-Bass, 1992), 12.

10. Schein, *Organizational Culture*, 17.

11. Schein, *Organizational Culture*, 8–10.

12. Harlan Cleveland, *Nobody in Charge: Essay on the Future of Leadership* (San Francisco, Jossey-Bass, 2002), 74.

13. Cleveland, *Nobody in Charge*, 74.

14. Cleveland, *Nobody in Charge*, 78.

15. Pam Pappas Stanoch, "Carrying Cultural Baggage," *Northwest Airlines World Traveler* (January 2001), 48.

16. Sarah Lawrence-Lightfoot, *Respect: An Exploration* (Reading, Mass.: Perseus Books, 1999), 13.

17. Laurent A. Park Daloz et al., *Common Fire: Leading Lives of Commitment in a Complex World* (Boston: Beacon Press, 1996), 76.

18. Peter Senge et al., *Schools That Learn: A Fifth Discipline Fieldbook for Educators, Parents, and Everyone Who Cares about Education* (New York: Doubleday Dell Publishing Group, 2000), 75–76.

19. Nicholas C. Burbules, *Dialogue in Teaching: Theory and Practice* (New York: Teachers College Press, 1993), 4.

20. Burbules, *Dialogue in Teaching*, 8.

21. Tullio Maranháo, ed., *The Interpretation of Dialogue* (Chicago: University of Chicago Press, 1990), 20.

22. Maranháo, ed., *Interpretation of Dialogue*, 21.

23. Daloz et al., *Common Fire*, 108.

24. Peter Block, *Stewardship: Choosing Service over Self-Interest* (San Francisco: Berrett-Koehler Publishers, 1993), 45.

25. Robert Terry, *Seven Zones for Leadership: Acting Authentically in Stability and Chaos* (Palo Alto, Calif.: Davies-Black Publishing, 2001), 191.

26. Terry, *Seven Zones for Leadership*, 192.

27. Block, *Stewardship*, xx.

28. Cleveland, *Nobody in Charge*, 43.

29. Cleveland, *Nobody in Charge*, 43.

30. Daloz et al., *Common Fire*, 3.

31. Cleveland, *Nobody in Charge*, 30.

CHAPTER 6

Change and the Future

THE DRIVING FORCE AND EFFECTS OF CHANGE

We never know if change will sweep in like a gentle breeze and seduce us with its promise or spin us around like a gale-force wind, knocking us off our feet and wreaking havoc everywhere. Either way, we don't really know the full effects of change until things calm down and some sort of order returns. Change causes us to examine our lives and sort through the experience, taking stock of its causes and effects. Sometimes we don't even recognize how much we have changed until later, long after the innovation or change event.

Change causes us to ask questions of leaders, such as, Why didn't you see it coming? Why didn't you protect us from it? Why wasn't it planned more carefully? It seems as if change is always a surprise, even when it is staring us in the face. It goes without saying that there are often multiple changes going on in our lives simultaneously, each adding to our potential for excitement and stress. When things go wrong or even when they go right, change takes its toll. People who experience deep change are sometimes called "survivors"—and for good reason. Change is a messy, complex, and seemingly permanent condition in our personal and professional lives.

I remember reading the best-selling book *Future Shock* by Alvin Toffler some years ago. Toffler described the way that people might react to change in the future. He thought we might need to create communities that would allow people to live as if they were living in an earlier time—essentially matching the pace of change with the capacity of people to adapt to it. He called these communities "enclaves of the

past—communities in which turnover, novelty, and choice are deliberately limited."[1] Toffler warned us about the accelerating pace of change
and its effects.

William Bridges warns of this dramatic shift when he says, "We are
still caught in the mid-twentieth-century-mindset, which conceived of
the main organizational problem as *the lack of change*."[2] Bridges goes
on to say that by the end of the twentieth century, the problem was not
the lack of change, but change itself. Bridges argues that change agents
aren't needed as much as change managers—those who know how to
help people transition through change.

*The fifth and last element of leadership, "change and the future,"
refers to the adjustment of people to change and its effects and the anticipated and actual effects of an innovation on the immediate and
long-term future of the group, organization, and community as nested
systems.* Leaders skilled in working with change understand the dynamics of change. They understand what happens under the surface
when change occurs, how it impacts people, culture, and systems, and
how change alters the future of organizations and communities.

WHY IS CHANGE SO HARD AND DANGEROUS?

Leaders engaged in change work understand that the nature of change
can vary dramatically and affect what type of leadership is needed.
Ronald Heifetz, author of *Leadership without Easy Answers*, distinguishes between adaptive and technical challenges. Technical challenges can be solved with existing knowledge and routine solutions.
Leaders with authority can provide the remedy. Adaptive challenges are
solved with learning, innovation, and action that "provokes debate, rethinking, and other processes of social learning" to locate a solution
that might work.[3] Heifetz defines leadership as "activity to mobilize
adaptation."[4]

When change requires more of us than what we want to give—our
time, energy, effort, power, sense of control, resources, and more—then
leadership is dangerous. "To lead is to live dangerously because when
leadership counts, when you lead people through difficult change, you
challenge what people hold dear—their daily habits, tools, loyalties,

and ways of thinking—with nothing more to offer than a possibility."[5] This kind of change throws us off balance and creates uncertainty, loss, and the potential reformulation of our professional lives.

Change is personal, even when it happens to us in our work lives. Leaders can estimate the potential danger of any change by imagining the effects a change will potentially have on people. A transformational change is a critical event or situation causing multiple changes in personal and organizational beliefs or values, relationships, ways of doing work, and more, with mostly unpredictable effects. Transformational change does not occur after the implementation of a linear strategic plan (where what exists is known and can be managed), but rather when the pressures of an ever changing environment force us to change. Many metaphors for change thought of in this way are derived from biology and use a systems approach; change involves complexity, and it can't be fully known or predicted at its inception.

No one can save us from change. I had a conversation about change with a group of twenty-five high school teachers. They were discussing the aspects of their system that were the most maddening examples of rules that worked against them and their mission to educate students. When I asked them why they did not change the system, they responded with a simple answer, "At least we know what it is and we have learned how to manipulate it."

They described the hours of anticipated conflict over changing anything (because one change can cause multiple changes) and the time and energy needed to redesign the system just wasn't worth it. They knew the system was inefficient and maddening, but they preferred a predictable and irrational environment to one that was one filled with potential conflict.

Changing the system involves a substantial investment of time and resources. We all suffer from "time poverty." Change involves a commitment of time and energy, and the payoff may not be worth it. Change may cause a vacuum in power, and few want to risk the loss of it. Sometimes it is intelligent to resist change because the proposed change is so problematic that it is unlikely to add much to the goal. There are plenty of reasons why we avoid change.

Leaders understand that engaging in a complex and transformative change is a time-consuming process. They must be aware of the dangers of change and the commitment that it requires. Even though we can't write the history and effects of a change effort ahead of time, we can understand what it takes to mobilize others to action. John Kotter describes the process of change as having eight steps:

1. Create a sense of urgency.
2. Put together a strong-enough team to direct the process.
3. Create an appropriate vision.
4. Communicate that new vision broadly.
5. Empower employees to act on the vision.
6. Produce sufficient short-term results to give their efforts credibility and to disempower the cynics.
7. Build momentum and use that momentum to tackle the tougher change problems.
8. Anchor the new behavior in organizational culture.[6]

Think about your experience with a change effort and look at the steps described above. Can you figure out what went wrong or what went right? Was the change effective, or were the costs so high that they outweighed its impact? The last change effort experienced by members predicts their attitude toward the next one. If the change effort was labor intensive and unsuccessful, resistance arises. One of the most damaging aspects of change is the wasted effort and the cost to people and organizations. When the influence of leadership "points in the wrong direction, in no direction despite rapid change, or along a reasonable trajectory at inadequate speed, the consequences can be tragic."[7]

Successful change leaders examine and frame a challenge or opportunity prior to taking action. They identify the factors that add dimension to a problem or opportunity, seek creative solutions, identify alternatives (including not responding to the problem), think systemically and collaboratively about the implications, and take action. Effective change leaders are aware of the dangers of leadership and monitor the process of change to ensure that its implementation costs don't exceed its potential.

If a change initiative results in gains and addresses a challenge that threatens the survival of the organization, the next effort may not be as difficult to manage. In a sense, leaders have the opportunity to create a culture of change over time when there are positive results. Perhaps the only way to prepare for change is to create a culture of change "producing the capacity to seek, critically assess, and selectively incorporate new ideas and practices—all the time, inside the organization as well as outside it."[8] Responsive cultures are deeply invested in continuous improvement and learning. The most proactive approach to change is organizational learning.

ORGANIZATIONAL LEARNING

Perhaps the most important asset of an organization is its people and their capacity to learn. One of the difficult issues associated with change is identifying what should never change (the things that make the organization great) and what must change because it does not support the future. Peter Senge, in his groundbreaking book *The Fifth Discipline: The Art and Practice of the Learning Organization*, identifies five new "component technologies" that are vital to learning organizations:

- *Systems thinking:* a conceptual framework, a body of knowledge and tools useful to identify the underlying patterns of systems
- *Personal mastery:* the process of clarifying a personal vision and making a commitment to accomplish what matters most
- *Mental models:* using inquiry to uncover the assumptions that influence our actions and holding them up to scrutiny
- *Building shared vision:* the process of unearthing a shared vision and purpose for the future
- *Team learning:* group interaction to transform thinking and take action through the process of dialogue and discussion[9]

These five human technologies offer a strategy for organizational change and renewal and help groups, organizations, and communities to look inside and discover barriers and opportunities. The concept behind organizational learning is the development of people. The role of the leader is to ensure that learning is a core strategy for ensuring the organization's success. The goals of learning involve knowledge building, analyzing systems, problem solving, and generating creative responses to the future. Much of what is experienced as organizational learning is obtained through a process of sharing collective wisdom and creating opportunities for people to develop new perspectives and understanding.

Organizational learning is linked to the pursuit of quality and excellence. The goal of quality is to improve both efficiency and effectiveness through collaboration and learning. This has changed the way people are organized (less management, flatter organizational structures) and the way employees are expected to work together (in teams for learning and change). There are many promising practices and technologies associated with organizational learning.

APPRECIATIVE INQUIRY

One of the most interesting organizational approaches to change is to turn the view of organizations upside down through appreciative inquiry (AI). Instead of thinking of an organization as "a problem to be solved," what if we thought about it as "a mystery to be embraced?"[10] AI has four cycles: (1) discovery, (2) dream, (3) design, and (4) destiny.[11] During discovery, questions are devised that move us toward the appreciation of "what is" and toward positive approaches to change. For example, we might ask a problem-and-deficit-focused question, such as, how can we eliminate racism or sexism? Or instead, we might ask an AI question, such as, how can we create a culture that values differences and ensures that everyone feels a sense of belonging?

AI pioneers believe that questions are critical to the direction and quality of the dialogue. The next two stages, dream and design, are about envisioning what might be and what should be—the ideal. Finally, destiny addresses the challenge of empowerment and learning. For many organizations, appreciative inquiry has replaced the strategic planning process as a nonlinear approach to cocreating the future.

The core technology of an AI approach is framing questions and orchestrating processes that lead to widespread participation in dialogue. AI leaders believe that the framing of the problem with the right questions sets the stage and determines the results of the process. Some advocate AI in addressing issues that are transglobal in scale. These "meetings" take advantage of the possibility of worldwide participation using the Internet. What if we had a worldwide conversation on hunger or violence? This is the future. Change is the forward motion into the future. What distinguishes the present from the future is change and, of course, time. How do we "prepare" for the future? Many concepts associated with transformational change apply to the future.

FUTURING

I saw a very disturbing science-fiction movie, *The Minority Report*, which painted a picture of the future that was both fascinating and frightening. Tom Cruise played the starring role of a police officer charged with arresting people for crimes that they would commit in the future, before they actually carried them out! The ability to "see" the future allowed people to prevent it. If you were to write a scenario of the future, what would it contain? What would be the source of your ideas? What process would you use to imagine the future? Peter Senge outlines three ways to think about the future:

1. Extrapolate, or think of the future as an extension of the past.
2. Imagine what might be, independent of what is.
3. Cultivate awareness and reflectiveness to be open to what is arising in the world and in us and continually ponder what matters most deeply to us.[12]

The key to thinking about the future according to Senge is to become more aware of the present (and how it came to be as it is). This is an interesting challenge. Some organizations engage in writing decision scenarios.[13] The Royal Dutch/Shell Group of companies uses this process. Decision scenarios are created as stories of what might occur over the coming years and decades and are developed after an extensive process of interviewing and research. The goal of decision scenarios is not to predict the future, but rather to prepare leaders by increasing their capacity to examine their "mental models" and gain new insights.

Harlan Cleveland describes the study of the future as "*imagining*— fashioning constructive alternative futures, then working backward from preferred outcomes to guide decisions about what we ought to be doing,

starting today, to bring them to pass."[14] Cleveland advocates this posi-
tivist approach because it promotes taking action on significant issues
that are complex and pose the greatest threat to survival, rather than
problem avoidance. Using this approach, everyone is a futurist because
we can all think about the present and take some action toward a preferred future. Try noticing some things about the present in your life and
imagine what they might mean.

NOTICING THE PRESENT

I recently was asked to think about the development of curriculum and
changes in the teaching-and-learning process for a school district engaged in futuristic strategic planning. They asked me to forecast some
educational changes in content, delivery, or teaching and learning over
the next twenty years and to present my ideas to an audience of educational and community stakeholders. I accepted the challenge and spent
hours thinking about it.

I noticed some things about the present that I thought might shape
the future. For example, "like-minds" software that is embedded in
some commercial Internet sites may change the delivery of education.
This software keeps track of your choices when you make a purchase
and offers you more of the same type of product the next time you log
on. Here's how it works. An online bookseller knows what you purchased in the past and offers you other books on the same subject the
next time you log on to your own personalized area of the screen. When
you select a book, you can also see the titles selected by people who
purchased the same books you did. And you know what—it works! I
inevitably purchase another book that comes to my attention because
my bookseller knows what I want.

What if this same software kept track of student interests or learning
styles and offered students more of what they like the next time they
logged on? Would it motivate them to learn more? Could the information be used to create an individualized profile that would be useful for
a teacher? How much more would students be inspired to learn if the
lessons were taught in their favorite "channels"?

Have you ever thought about Oprah Winfrey as a leading national educator? Just visit her website (www.oprah.com) and see how she is

transforming parent and person education. What if visitors to Oprah's site were to encounter school resources and lessons customized for their children? Would this become a new way to encourage family learning?

Recently I read an article about the intention of the Massachusetts Institute of Technology (MIT) to offer all of its content online at no cost.[15] This includes course outlines, lecture notes, reading lists, assignments, and more. The goal is to create a global web of knowledge and to encourage other institutions to do the same. Since courses are proprietary and are an asset of institutions of higher education, this bold step is a marked departure from the current direction of creating "firewalls" so that outsiders don't have access to courses. What does this mean, and why did MIT decide to make this move? What is MIT thinking that is markedly different from what others in the same field are thinking? Issues about knowledge, control, access, delivery, and choice are dominant themes in education. What is the potential gain from giving knowledge away?

Futuring is a creative process and involves finding new ways to "see" the future by studying the present and applying some imagination. There's no wrong way to think about the future except to ignore it! Leaders as futurists focus the attention of people and organizations on developing a shared vision and direction and mobilizing people to action. Leadership is a process, activity, and survival strategy for the future.

As an element of leadership, change and the future influence the way that we explain the past, interpret the present, and approach the future. Leadership is an activity that engages us in "change work," providing a process to navigate the present and propelling us to move into the future. Using your knowledge about change and the future can help you expand your "frame" for thinking about any situation and what leaders and members do to build community. Part II of this book, "Applying the Elements of Leadership," describes the challenges of leadership and some potential ways to "frame" these experiences.

NOTES

1. Alvin Toffler, *Future Shock* (New York: Random House, 1970), 346.

2. William Bridges, *Managing Transitions: Making the Most of Change* (Reading, Mass.: Addison-Wesley, 1991), 123.

3. Ronald A. Heifetz, *Leadership without Easy Answers* (Cambridge, Mass.: Harvard University Press, 1994), 87.

4. Heifetz, *Leadership without Easy Answers*, 27.

5. Ronald A. Heifetz and Marty Linsky, *Leadership on the Line: Staying Alive through the Dangers of Leading* (Boston: Harvard Business School Press, 2002), 2.

6. John P. Kotter, *John P. Kotter on What Leaders Really Do* (Boston: Harvard Business School Press, 1999), 7.

7. Kotter, *John P. Kotter*, 2.

8. Michael Fullan, *Leading in a Culture of Change* (San Francisco: Jossey-Bass, 2001), 44.

9. Peter M. Senge, *The Fifth Discipline: The Art and Practice of the Learning Organization* (New York: Doubleday Currency, 1990), 6–10.

10. David L. Cooperrider et al., eds., *Appreciative Inquiry: Rethinking Human Organization toward a Positive Theory of Change* (Champaign, Ill.: Stipes Publishing, 2000), 23.

11. Cooperrider et al., eds., *Appreciative Inquiry*, 9–16.

12. Marianne Willliamson, ed., *Imagine What America Could Be in the 21st Century: Visions of a Better Future from Leading American Thinkers* (New York: New American Library, 2000), 175.

13. Joseph Jaworski, *Synchronicity: The Inner Path of Leadership* (San Francisco: Berrett-Koehler Publishers, 1998), 140.

14. Harlan Cleveland, *Nobody in Charge: Essays on the Future of Leadership* (San Francisco: Jossey-Bass, 2002), 132.

15. Jan Dempsey, "MIT Breaks New Ground by Offering Free Online Courses," in the *Minneapolis Star Tribune*, November 12, 2002, E9.

CHAPTER 7

Discovering the Authentic Leader in You

Your success as a leader depends somewhat on your success as a human being.

YOU ARE THE LEADER OF YOUR LIFE

You grow as a leader based on the choices you make and the knowledge and skills that you gain from the experience of life. When you are leading your life (and not allowing the events of your life to lead you), you promote your learning and development. You prepare for the experience of leadership by developing your knowledge and talents. Learning how to get along with others and successfully navigating life's challenges contributes to your preparation for leadership. This process starts in childhood and continues through adulthood.

When you are a leader in your life, your initial focus is on your personal well-being and development as an individual. When you are a leader of others, your focus is on the development and success of others without abandoning your authentic self. *Your life and what you have learned from living your life are your leadership capacity*. This capacity grows as you expand your knowledge and experience and learn to put your talents to work for others as a leader. Preparing for a leadership role involves the inner work of self-discovery and reflection. You must invest the time to understand what makes up the authentic you and what you have to offer in service to others.

Effective leaders have (1) a *vision and guiding values*, (2) effective *interpersonal skills and group facilitation strategies* to work with people,

(3) high levels of *self-awareness and self-mastery* to appraise their own performance, learn, and change, and (4) a genuine *desire to make a difference* in the lives of people. Most of these gifts and talents are characteristic of mature and self-actualized individuals who are leaders of their lives. Your success as a leader depends somewhat on your success as a human being. Mature people have vision, values, effective interpersonal skills, and so on. There is more to leadership than the role, position, or general characteristics of leaders and what they do—there is also the authentic "you" that you bring to leadership.

LEADERSHIP AND AUTHENTICITY

The way you work with and lead others is unique to you. The authentic leader within you is revealed when you lead in a way that is natural to you and incorporates your personal mission, values, beliefs, passions, talents, interests, strengths, and experience. Another definition of leadership is that it is the outward expression of the authentic you that you give in service to others. Authentic leaders look inward to assess their motivations, potential, and experience, and they look outward for opportunities to lead in ways that are consistent with their internal world. Being authentic means discovering the real you—who you are, what you can do, and how you can continue to develop as a human being, leader, and member of many groups.

The "welcoming promise of authenticity" is expressed this way: "That which is true and real inside and outside us is worthy and deserving of commitment and service."[1] One facet of authentic leadership is the authentic leader in you. Russ Moxley describes the authentic leader:

> Being authentic is knowing ourselves and being ourselves as we engage others in the activity of leadership—no playing games, no acting, no fulfilling the expectations of others. We are actually and exactly who we are. Nothing false, nothing imitative, nothing imaginary. Being authentic means not hiding behind the mask, not faking what we think and feel, not using spin to promote a sanitized version of the truth.[2]

As a leader, you must know and be true to your authentic self. Your first step in discovering the authentic you is to take stock of your leadership assets by assessing your development and growth as the leader of your life. You might think of your life as the first course in your leadership development. Your life history is made up of your experience and the choices you have made to transform your potential into the visible talents and strengths that you offer to others as a leader.

YOUR LEADERSHIP PLATFORM

Students in my introductory graduate-level class on leadership and organizational theory incorporate their ideas about leadership into their "leadership platform." The leadership platform represents their knowledge and preparation for leadership. It is a symbolic home for their new and emerging ideas about leadership. Their ideas, values, and life experiences are the foundation for their leadership and serve as a platform for their actions as leaders and participants in leadership. They present this platform to the members of their class as a culminating activity. Here is Virgil Jones's story.

Jones's leadership story is centered on his family, his early life of poverty, and his struggle to succeed. He left home at age thirteen. As he was leaving home, his grandmother said to him, "When you take the name of this family with you, you bring it back the same way." He explained this by telling us, "When you are poor, the only thing that you own is your family name, your word, and your reputation. That's all you've got and so it's important."

Jones is a self-starter and achiever. He struggled against poverty, against prejudice, and against all odds—and he achieved. His success is due to his extra effort and willingness to learn. He says that he had to run faster to catch up because his life circumstances put him behind. Jones, now twenty-nine years old, knows his mission. He wants to help disadvantaged youth with their struggle. His idea of leadership is that he must be honest and real with others. Jones tells us about his authentic leadership when he says, "I don't want to be a role model, I want to be a real model." He has moral authority because he did it the hard way, and this is how he intends to lead. How do you intend to lead? What is the source of your passion? How does your life experience relate to leadership?

You can discover the raw material for leadership by examining the critical life events and milestones that define who you are and determining how they relate to your view of leadership. Try sorting through many definitions of leadership and figure out what leadership means for you at this stage and place in your life. When my students share their leadership platform, they explain what they know about their capacity to lead others and how they want to grow toward leadership. At the culmination of this journey, students realize that this project asks them to discover and share the "authentic you" that they bring to leadership. The theme of authenticity in leadership is central to your success as a leader and to identifying what you can bring to leadership.

The developmental challenges of childhood are similar to the developmental challenges of leaders. You develop your leadership identity by forming relationships, learning how to learn, working with others to accomplish the goals of the organization, and accepting responsibility for your choices and actions. Becoming a leader is a continuous developmental process of discovery, growth, and maturation—we are continually "in process" as adults and leaders.

YOUR LIFE MAP

Your life map can help you identify the experiences in your life that have shaped your character and defined the person you are today. Leadership is a social process and is defined by the relationship between leaders and members. Mature leaders are self-aware. They know how their life history has influenced them. They are able to stand outside of themselves and examine their relationships with others. This understanding of "self" and "other" is essential to the formation of our identity as individuals and central to the role of leadership.

Your life map is your personal record of the challenges you have faced and survived and the routes you have selected to develop your talents. Take some time to construct your life map by considering all the things that have had an impact on you and your development. One way of thinking about your life map is to imagine that you are holding a deck of cards in your hands and each card represents one episode or event in your life that was meaningful. Instead of four suits (hearts, clubs, diamonds, and spades), there are six different suits. The life card suits are (1) family and relationship history, (2) life factors, (3) milestones, (4) critical life events, (5) peak learning experiences, and (6) influential people.

Imagine that you are sitting opposite a confidential friend or family member who is vitally interested in you and willing to give you his or her undivided attention. Prepare for your meeting with your confidant by selecting a life card. Think about the important moments in your life that have influenced the person and leader you are today. Look at the description and questions for each card and have a dialogue with yourself or another person.

YOUR FAMILY AND RELATIONSHIP HISTORY

When you draw a family and relationship history life card, think about your experience as a child, sibling, student, spouse, parent, friend, coworker, or community member. *Your family and relationship history is made up of your experience relating to and interacting with others during your formative and adult years*. Describe your experience to a real or imagined listener by sharing a story about something that had an impact on you and shaped your ideas about leadership. It is not the story itself that is important but how you *interpret* and *integrate* the meaning of your experience to explain the person and leader you are today. Yannita is an African American woman with a life history of taking responsibility for others. Here is her story:

> I was the oldest child in my family, and I was often left in charge of my siblings while my mother worked to support the family. I found out right away that it doesn't work to try to boss your brothers and sisters. I had to persuade them to behave by negotiating with them every day. I made sure that everyone got something out of a situation—including me! This early experience is one of the reasons why I am a successful union leader today. The management representatives on the other side of the table don't come close to the trouble that my younger brotherss and sisters could raise with me. I sometimes look at the people across the table during negotiations and think, "If I could get my younger brothers and sisters to mind me all those years ago, I am going to get something from you today!"

FAMILY AND RELATIONSHIPS DIALOGUE QUESTIONS

1. What did your experience as a family member teach you about relationships? What stories illustrate this lesson?
2. How did your childhood relationships with people outside of your family influence you? What positive and negative experiences shaped your learning?
3. How have your adult relationships with friends, colleagues, and lovers shaped the way you interact with and relate to others?

LIFE FACTORS

Your education, spiritual upbringing, and membership in a community may have had a major influence on your development. Life factors such as race, ethnicity, religion, country of origin, place and date of birth, medical history, mobility, gender, social and economic status, and sexual orientation are part of you and your development. The presence and influence of life factors might explain the source of some of your values and principles. Life factors can be an advantage or disadvantage and propel us to seek challenges or retreat from them. You never know what role a life factor played in someone else's life—it is how they interpret the influence that counts.

One life factor is gender. Both males and females are often discouraged from entering certain occupations or professions due to stereotypes about "appropriate" work roles for men and women. This is slowly changing. It takes a lot of effort to counteract cultural stereotypes about work roles, particularly when there seems to be little variance in some occupations or positions. Many barriers still exist for women and people of color in getting appointed or promoted to the highest levels of management in government, business, and education. The life factor of gender may have influenced some people to work harder at climbing the ladder of success or held others back from aspiring to a leadership role. Here is Sally's story:

> When I was in elementary school, my fifth-grade teacher introduced a fire-safety project. The goal of the project was to learn about fire prevention by having a contest. Each student completed projects and earned

merit badges. The student with the most merit badges would be appointed fire chief. Filled with determination, I went home and went right to work on the projects. Each day I checked the chart on the wall to see if I was still in the top position with the highest number of merit badges. When the contest ended, I was relieved and excited to see that I had earned the most badges. The winner of the contest was announced at the end of the day. A male student with fewer badges won. I must have looked pretty upset because I remember the teacher explaining to the class that fire chiefs were male. I was awarded the title of "assistant" fire chief.

Putting on a brave front, I made it through the rest of the day without breaking down, and that was a struggle. It was my first experience with blatant sexism. The lesson that I learned was that I would have to earn many more merit badges than the nearest competitor to compete for jobs that are traditionally held by men. Now that I am a leader, I want to make sure that people are promoted on merit and not for any other reason.

Try to identify the life factors that are the most significant in your development. How do these factors play into your ideas about leadership? How have your experiences influenced how you relate to or interact with others or fueled your motivation to lead?

MILESTONES

A milestone is a developmental landmark on your life map when you achieved a significant goal. Your achievement of goals is important to the development of your identity because it shows that you can achieve what you set out to do and you are aware of both the *process* and the *price* of success. Some examples of milestones are graduation from high school or college, getting your first job, or moving away from home. Achieving a goal requires vision, strategy, persistence, energy, commitment, and sustained effort.

Most milestones represent a significant accomplishment. These can be defining moments in your personal or professional life and contribute to your confidence as a leader. Your payoff for accomplishing goals is increased knowledge, wisdom, and visible success, and the acquisition of emotional and tactical resources for future use.

Emotional and tactical resources are useful to you because they help you to meet the next challenge. You know you have what it takes to succeed. You can develop the resilience of a long-distance runner who runs a marathon when you have struggled to achieve a major goal. Successful leaders have a quality of "stick-to-it-ness" that inspires confidence. People want to know about your track record and personal best. They also want to know that you have tried, failed, and learned from your mistakes. People expect their leaders to be marathon runners and go the distance.

CRITICAL LIFE EVENTS

Another important element of your life map is critical life events. *A critical life event is an experience that results in significant learning, growth, and change.* An example of a critical life event might be the death of a parent or the loss of a dear friend. The critical life event becomes a transformative experience when your perspective or goals change as a result of this event. Parents who have lost a child due to an illness may use their grief to dedicate themselves to raising money for a cure. The Wetterling family lost their son Jacob to a kidnapper in St. Cloud, Minnesota, and started a foundation to help other families find their loved ones. Critical life events transform people's mission and goals and often create an opportunity for leadership abilities to emerge.

Critical life events may influence the choice of a career or a change in your values or relationships. Some children who watch a parent die from an illness enter the medical profession to help others. The lessons that are learned from critical life events can have a lasting impact on your development or values. A terrifying experience with a playground bully who caused you to suffer or the isolation you may have felt on the first day of school may be the source and motivation of your empathy and compassion for others. This experience may motivate you to make sure that others are physically and psychologically safe or cause you to become a mentor to a new employee during his or her first year of employment. Another critical life event may be the day you met your best friend or the experience of moving to a new community. It marks a place where a single event or several connected events had a lasting impact on your development.

The destruction of the Twin Towers in New York City on 9-11-01 was a critical life event for many people and an entire nation. It is not the event itself (horrific as it was), but how people interpret the meaning of the event for themselves and others that makes it a transformative event. There may be an immediate awareness of its impact, or it may take years to fully understand. This experience has fundamentally changed how some people view themselves as people and their place in the world. It may have altered some thoughts about the future and caused people to examine the relative importance of the others and the material things in our lives. The 9-11-01 attack created a sense of loss and marked a period of dramatic change in many lives. What is the influence of this critical event and how have you learned, grown, or changed as a result of this experience? What impact do you think this event may have on your role as a leader or your ideas about leadership?

PEAK LEARNING EXPERIENCES

Another influential factor on your life map may be a peak learning experience. *A peak learning experience stirs your interests, emotions, and understanding as a result of a powerful episode of learning.* Peak learning experiences are easily recalled in great detail. You can recall the setting, the people who were there, what happened, and how it affected you. Peak learning experiences create opportunities for deep learning and often point the way to a future career choice. Many times these episodes occur in school or through the guidance of a coach, teacher, parent, or mentor. Suddenly the world of learning opens up, and we find that there is more to know and explore.

An employee who participates in the challenge of riding whitewater rapids or conquering a difficult rope course as a team member may be experiencing a peak learning experience. The learner is deeply involved emotionally and cognitively in the episode and connected to others in a way that was not possible before the event. The experience may move you beyond words and provide you with new information about your interests and capacities.

When I was in high school, my eleventh-grade history teacher challenged me to explain why the British should have won the American War of Independence. I remember thinking that the topic was impossible and tried to change the assignment. Despite my protests, the teacher prevailed, and I was stuck with the subject of my research project. I took the bus downtown alone (another defining moment) and tried to find any source that might help me answer the question of the research paper. I spent the day lost in the stacks of the city's largest library in downtown Minneapolis. I can still vividly recall the smell and feel of the dusty books. I just sat on the floor and pulled out nearly every book that might help me. When I found information that supported my emerging theory of why the British should have won the War of Independence (and didn't), I silently shouted, yes!

Peak learning experiences teach us something about ourselves and what we are capable of learning. I learned that I could develop a theory that was not published in a book and that scholarship required investigation and inventiveness. I could be a scholar! My life changed that year, and suddenly I couldn't wait to get out of high school and start college. A peak learning experience can happen at any time in your life when you experience a state of optimal learning and suddenly new doors are opened for your mind and spirit.

INFLUENTIAL PEOPLE

Influential people are also located on your life map. *Influential people guide you through tough and challenging moments, provide you with support, and serve as an example of who you might become some day*. Sometimes the influential person does not appear until we are ready to learn. You can learn by his or her coaching and example. Locate the influential people in your life on your life map. List parents, teachers, family members, friends, and outstanding leaders who served as your guides and mentors. They are partially responsible for your success. Parents are often the most significant people in our lives.

Chang is from Cambodia, and he talks about his father as the most influential person in his life. He related to me that his father was a minister and a well-respected member of the clan. His father was a friend and role model to all people in his community. He believed in the idea of community and brought this sense of community to the United

States from Cambodia. This influence inspired Chang to strive to be a leader in his community.

YOUR LIFE MAP

Milestones, critical events, peak learning experiences, mentors, and guides make up the story of your personal and leadership identity. It is what makes up the authentic you that you offer to others as a leader. These are the historical markers on your life map. You must pull off the road to figure out what happened to you, what you learned, and what it means in your life. After your life map is completed, your task is to interpret the journey, share it with others, and discover the authentic you. You will explore your life journey by creating your life map. The life map is a tool to help you identify the impact of the critical events of your life up to now and to identify how these experiences have shaped you as a leader.

Your life map is a graphic representation of your individual development. The life map is a metaphor and a tool to help you sort through your life and your leadership journey up to now. Your life map is filled with the experiences in your life in chronological order that explain you. Think back on your life and identify the stages and accomplishments of your life. Think about your milestones, critical events, family and friendship history, peak learning experiences, and personal mentors and guides. Use the idea of a life map to begin your personal narrative or story about your leadership. What do these experiences mean to you, and how do you relate this to leadership? If you presented your leadership platform, how would you share it with others? Do you know what motivates you to lead?

Mature and maturing human beings are engaged in the continuous process of learning. Your progress through the stages of adult development is a factor in your personal and professional success. The discovery of your authentic self is partially accomplished through a process of feedback, introspection, change, and reflection. Successful leaders are reflective leaders and use self-assessment and feedback from others to improve and learn. This allows them to reveal their authentic selves to others. In the next chapter, the challenges of transitioning to leadership are described.

NOTES

1. Robert Terry, *Seven Zones for Leadership: Acting Authentically in Stability and Chaos* (Palo Alto, Calif.: Davies-Black Publishing, 2001), 418.

2. Russ S. Moxley, *Leadership and Spirit: Breathing New Vitality and Energy into Individuals and Organizations* (San Francisco: Jossey-Bass, 2000), 126.

CHAPTER 8

Transitioning to Leadership

How can transition create a new beginning?

TRANSITION IS A CHANGE EVENT

Transition is *the adjustment that people go through to respond to a significant change*. Successful leaders are aware of the challenges and opportunities associated with transitioning into a new leadership role. Changes in personnel, processes, or practices result in a predictable period of instability, loss, and challenge. Effective leaders are committed to the success of people and the organization, as well as their own success, during times of instability and change. As a result of the challenges associated with a major change, there is considerable opportunity for new learning for everyone involved during transition. If the idea of leadership is to develop the capacity of others to contribute, then there is room for everyone to grow in the organization. This should be your central message!

Transition is one of the most important events in your future success, and it begins before you ever take over your new role or assignment. The appointment of a leader or manager to a new position is a significant change event. Transition can be a crippling or an energizing experience based on a number of factors. The core issues that people are often concerned about during transition are changes in personnel or practice and the anticipated impact on them and their work role(s). People can tolerate some change with good communication and support, as long as some aspects of their current role or work assignments remain the same. If there are organizational changes that are significant and substantive changes in leadership focus and style, the period of transition is likely to be difficult and to take more time to reach a period of stabilization. There will be considerable "storming" and chaos before stability is restored.

The circumstances of a personnel change are important to understand before taking on a new role. Ask the following questions: Why is this position currently available? What is the history of this position? What happened to my predecessor? What are the expectations for this position (build on success or shake things up)? If this is a new position, why was it created and what are the expectations for it? If your succession to a new leadership role is due to the normal conditions of retirement or promotion, then the period of transition may be relatively short. However, if your appointment results from the poor performance of the previous leader or a failing track record of organizational performance, the period of transition is likely to be more challenging and is often extended.

The knowledge you acquire before assuming the new position and your sensitivity with regard to your appointment and your predecessor(s) can impact the productivity and morale of employees over the next few years. Leaders in transition must respect the history and contribution of all past employees (including leaders) no matter how great or small. Never highlight or focus on the mistakes of others. Whatever the organization is today, the mere fact that it still exists and has delivered some product or service to others over time is worthy of acknowledgment. Regarding your predecessor, almost everyone has some supporters and successes. Take the high road, be gracious, thank people for their service, and focus on the task at hand—while getting to know people and setting the direction for the future.

During transition there are shifts in power and influence that may impact employees. Those who were influential with the former supervisor may fear the loss of their power and access to resources and rewards. The leader's departure causes a shift in the balance of power among employees. Some employees will perceive this as a loss, while others may look upon the change as a new opportunity. Sometimes a change in leadership results in little more than a new signature on purchase orders. The same "players" may retain their favored status with the new regime. In other cases, a change in leadership may result in sweeping changes in roles, expectations, responsibilities, goals, and even the employment status or fortunes of some employees.

Many employees fear transition because of its unpredictability—the status quo is preferred because at least employees know what it is and where they stand in the organization. A change in leadership may cause some employees to reduce their involvement or return to former and less-favored practices involving less work and effort. Major initiatives are likely to stall until the new leader or manager assumes the new position. No one wants to waste any effort on a project that may not be supported or take a risk and fail.

As a leader in transition, you will be learning, and so will everyone else. If you aren't careful, you can make some early mistakes that will be difficult to repair. You may fail to understand the context of your new environment and make hasty decisions that are not useful or appreciated. You can avoid this early and obvious mistake by learning as much as you can about people and the organization. No one expects you to understand everything immediately, and you can use the early stages of leadership transition to listen and learn.

Your primary goal is to learn as much as you can and withhold judgment about people and the culture of the organization until you have an "insider's" knowledge of how things work. Become a detective and find out as much as you can. Look beneath the surface and identify the reasons for current practices. Do an audit of the culture and find out what is highly valued, sacred, and significant. Learn about the "rituals" that are meaningful to people and the heroes and heroines who have made a difference in the organization. Ask a lot of questions and take notes. Share what you have learned, and ask others if your information or initial impressions are correct.

When you look into an imaginary mirror of the organization, you should see the reflection of all its past and present employees and their contributions. Remember that we all work in the shadow of those who were there before us, or because of the early efforts of founders, community members, or investors who helped an idea become a reality. Before charging ahead, learn about the past and the current reality as others describe it, and appreciate their contributions.

THE POLITICS OF TRANSITION

Since taking on a new leadership role is political, alliances may be formed too early, before the leader understands enough to make good decisions. People form alliances or use influence tactics to respond to the vacuum of power and influence that is created when the leader departs. Effective leaders avoid alliances and don't make deals that result in a competitive win-lose environment. Long-established bureaucratic organizations are likely to be highly political, and the process of making decisions and allocating resources can be complex and inefficient.

Use your political radar and identify the diverse needs and concerns of key people and groups. This will help you understand the context for your leadership and identify ways that you can successfully gain support for it. Understanding the political environment doesn't compromise your leadership unless you decide to base decisions on politics rather than on effective practice. Negotiating a political environment helps you to identify the potential opposition to a future direction or discover ways to meet the needs of competing factions.

THE FOOTPRINTS OF LEADERSHIP—YOU AND YOUR PREDECESSOR'S ACTIONS

When you transition to a new role, there is always the shadow of your past and your predecessor's shadow as well. Your past is your personal and professional reputation and your career track record. Whether you are promoted from within an organization or you make a change in location, everyone has a shadow. This shadow includes your past success and failures in your previous careers. Your first opportunity to acknowledge this past is during the interview. If you have some successes, claim them and share the credit with others. If you had some failures, describe them and discuss what you will do differently in the future.

Whatever you do, don't wait until you are on the job before acknowledging the mistakes. Your mistakes and disappointing areas of performance are your areas of vulnerability and will surface when you have to make difficult and unpopular decisions. Tell the truth and acknowledge your past during the interview—this will reduce its impact in the future because it is not news anymore. These past mistakes and failures are your "baggage," and everyone has some of it.

Dr. Elaine Bauman, principal of River Falls High School in River Falls, Wisconsin, talked to me about the "baggage" of candidates during a search process to fill an opening for an assistant principal. She said, "We all carry baggage from our past. If you are part of the school district and promoted from within, you have already unpacked your baggage and we know what it is. If you are from somewhere else, sooner or later you will have your baggage as well. It is just easier to get the job when you are from the outside because we haven't seen your baggage yet."

If you failed to disclose some of your mistakes during the interview process, look for opportunities to share these mistakes during the first six months of your transition. Sooner or later, your successes and mistakes will follow you. You don't need to declare your success, but you do need to declare some of your mistakes. Examples of mistakes might be poor decisions, lack of acceptable performance in a job, or a mistake you made in communication with an employee, parent, or stakeholder. Be honest, open up a little, and let people know that you are willing to be accountable for your success and mistakes.

ORGANIZATIONAL MATCH—WHAT'S YOUR FIT?

The "organizational match" between the leader and the organization is an assessment about the leader's fitness and qualifications for the position and whether or not he or she exhibits the qualities of an ideal employee in that particular organization. Generally people are selected for a leadership role because in some way they represent the organizational "ideal" of a valuable employee. People select leaders who are like them and have similar values and goals for the organization. During the selection process, there is an assessment about whether or not the candidate is the right "fit" for the position and the organization. Those involved in the hiring process want to know if you have the knowledge, skills, and experience to be successful. If this assessment is positive, then the next test for selection is whether you fit the organizational ideal.

For example, if your organization has a strong "family" culture, then you may have been selected because you were friendly and spoke highly of the importance of people. If you were hired in a very technical organization, you may have been selected because of your expertise and obvious demonstration of professionalism. You may have been selected because one goal during the selection process was to recruit people who add diversity to the organization, in either their experience or their qualities. If you were hired because you are different from others, your challenge is to find how the organizational ideal can be expanded to include you and offer more future opportunities for people with a diversity of backgrounds, experiences, and qualities.

Many individuals describe the challenge of "token" status and the difficulty of being singled out as a representative of a group rather than as themselves. This concern is legitimate and poses some added challenges to transition. Often the first people who break a stereotype report that they feel like they are swimming in a fish bowl where all of their actions are on constant display. They struggle to be seen as individuals and not members of an underrepresented, or "protected," class. No one can realistically represent anyone but himself or herself. For example, if you are the first female in a male-dominated role, the cultural expectations and stereotypes associated with gender bias will come into play. How can you be assertive without being viewed as aggressive and unfeminine?

If you are significantly different from the other candidates and you are selected for the position, your transition may command more attention, and in some ways, your entrance plan may involve the education of others. You will struggle initially to be known as an individual and not as a representative of a group. Your qualifications or background may be viewed with greater scrutiny. This is not right, but it may happen, and you need to prepare for it. You may wish to comfort yourself with the knowledge that you are paving the way for others to follow you (an act of leadership).

Some organizations assign mentors to help leaders successfully transition to a leadership role. This mentor shares information about the informal rules regarding how things work and how to get things done and provides access and introduction to the social and informal networks of the organization. A mentor can help you if he or she is well connected and respected. If there isn't a mentor available to you, you may have to recruit one. Take your time and find someone who is skilled, credible, and willing to help you.

If your professional background is not typical, you will want to acquire as much knowledge as you can about the core areas of production or service and then lend the areas of your expertise to the organization as added value. Some school districts have recently hired people with a military or business background to serve as principals or superintendents. This background can add a dimension to leadership, but you cannot substitute this knowledge for understanding the fundamentals regarding teaching and learning.

You may want to think about why you were hired and what others expect of you in this new position and then see if you want to accept and face the challenges and opportunities that are ahead because of your unique qualities. This is the authentic you that you bring to the leadership role. Your challenge is to bring the authentic you into your formula for success as a leader and use your unique qualities to address the goals of transition described in the next section.

TRANSITION GOALS

The leader in transition sets in motion a process to define reality and set the direction for the future. There is a special leadership agenda for the early stages of your transition, generally the first six months. The goal of your agenda and entrance plan for leadership is to assess the current reality, determine how you can contribute, determine the future direction, and build a base of support for your actions as leader. Leaders influence and persuade others to support the goals of the organization by understanding what is needed and by influencing people to work toward the achievement of goals. These goals should benefit people and the organization. If this goal-setting process is accomplished successfully, it can set the stage for your future success as a leader. Unfortunately, some leaders are focused on their own success as the main event, and this can result in a predictable loss of credibility. Make sure your motives and your goals are designed for the success of others and the organization—not to feather your own nest or career.

Successful leaders take the time to build relationships with people and earn their support. They ask for input, gather data, build a base of support, and intelligently determine the actions that will result in positive and productive change. During transition, the leader does the following:

1. Develops a leadership entrance plan to get to know people and the organization and build relationships to gain the trust and support of others
2. Identifies the key stakeholders and establishes a communication plan to learn various perspectives, establishing positive patterns of interaction
3. Takes stock of the current state of the organization, using all of the data that is available, including information from people at all levels of the organization
4. Locates and defines core services and products and identifies any areas that appear inconsistent or off course from the core services
5. Assesses the current stage of development of the organization (essentially comparing the current state to existing practices within the field)
6. Works with others to agree on a future direction and establishes goals
7. Persuades others to renew their commitment to the success of each other, the organization, and the external stakeholders, customers, and community

YOUR ENTRANCE PLAN FOR LEADERSHIP

Your first step is to develop your "entrance plan" for leadership. This process begins before you actually start your new position. Your leadership entrance plan is your action plan for gaining support. It identifies your strategies to (1) assume the role of leader, (2) establish relationships and gain the support of people, and (3) establish the future direction of your department, team, or organization. One important component of your leadership entrance plan is the message that you wish to communicate to others about your leadership. This message describes your reasons for joining the organization or department, your professional goals, your guiding values as a leader, and the way you intend to work with people. This is your guiding theory and should reflect the authentic leader in you.

If you are passionately committed to education and children, then share your passion with others. If you want to support the success of others by developing their talents, let them know that is your goal and ask people about their talents. If you have a track record of success in your organization, field, or both and you are motivated by a drive for excellence, describe your vision of excellence to others. If you want to contribute by building a team and developing a network to support the work of others, tell people that and start building a team. Don't make your leadership a mystery. Let others know what motivates you to lead and ask them for help.

The selection of symbolic acts to portray your leadership to others is critical and should be consistent with your leadership message. The people you meet, the way you allocate your time, your appearance and style, and the way you communicate will either affirm or create confusion about your leadership. If people are important to you, then show up at their events. Wear business attire if you want to convey formality and professionalism. If you are in a small town, you may want to wear clothing that is defined as "business casual wear" so that you appear approachable and friendly. If you spend too much time reviewing data and not meeting people, you will send a message about what is important to you. If you talk too much and fail to take the time to ask questions and observe how things work, you will be viewed as self-absorbed.

You can be authentic and still do what is needed during transition— talk to people, study the organization, and let people see the expertise and qualities that you bring to the position. You cannot lead without the support of members, and the key to your success is to gain their trust and support. Members give you the opportunity to lead when you provide help and offer hope about the future. Get to know people, how the organization works, and how you can contribute.

YOUR ACTIONS SPEAK VOLUMES ABOUT YOU

Think about how you intend to spend the first few hours and days in your new position. How will you convey your central message about your leadership? Give yourself a leadership audit by thinking about your response to the following question: are your actions consistent with your core values and the authentic you? This is a time to lead with your head and your heart. Think about the elements of your message that you want to communicate, select sincere and appropriate actions that are consistent with your core values, meet people from all stakeholder groups, and give something of yourself to gain the cooperation of others.

One of the biggest challenges in transition is that people will formulate a theory about what kind of a leader you are from your early actions, and this is the time when mistakes are likely to be high. Desiring to be viewed as an effective, "take charge" leader, some may make decisions and take action prematurely. Using a "command" style, rather than a participatory style, can be dangerous to your future success. A problem may be solved in the short term with a satisfactory result but may cause retreat and withdrawal of employees in the long run. On the other hand, if the problem has been of long standing and a decision gets made that eliminates the drain on the time and energy of people and resources, you may be viewed very positively.

If you are an action-oriented leader, you may want to naturally dig in and solve as many problems as you can without recognizing that you may leave others behind with your quick actions. If you are a deliberative leader, you will want to take your time to respond to issues after a thorough analysis. You may miss an obvious opportunity for streamlining a process or improving a dysfunctional situation with decisive action. Your challenge as a leader is to use your intelligence and good judgment to determine what is needed. This process involves understanding the context and situational demands of a decision and the costs and implications of your decision-making style and strategies. To the degree that it is possible, evaluating your decisions and actions before you make them is very critical in the early months of your leadership. Later on, decisions get easier because you understand people and the constraints and possibilities for your leadership.

Initially, your lack of knowledge and experience of the particular setting limit your ability to make a fully informed decision, so the chances of making a poor decision in the early stages of your leadership are high. Take at least a little time to examine a problem, consider alternative solutions, and make a good decision. If you act quickly and without the involvement of others, will that action solve the problem and gain support? If you fail to act, will the safety of others be compromised and result in your failure in a core area of leadership—the safety of others and the preservation of assets? These questions get to the heart of intelligent action and strategic leadership.

The goal of a strategic leader is to work with others to solve problems effectively and to live to lead another day while staying consistent with personal and professional ethics and professional standards of practice. Strategic leaders want to be effective, deliver consistent and high-quality results, and reduce their risk taking (to the degree possible) in a role filled with contradictions and sometimes unreasonable expectations.

The reduction of risk is a matter of strategic thinking and intelligent action and incorporates your common sense, experience, and knowledge of the standards of professional practice. This is a tall order, and learning to apply sophisticated decision-making rules and strategic thinking to the core functions of leadership is a developmental task. We learn from our own actions and what we can observe and learn from others. If you are the type that likes to "shoot from the hip," eventually you are going to take too many falls. Leaders take the time to think through their decisions but act swiftly when necessary. Find a mentor, read books, and stay open to understanding and reflecting on your experience.

During the early weeks or months of your new role, you have not yet earned the trust of your members. Remember that a member is anyone (including you) who temporarily agrees to be influenced and supports the goals that will meet their needs and the needs of the organization. It is their gift to you and can be revoked at any time. The decisions you make and the ways you involve or choose not to involve others in the process of leadership provide people with information about your leadership style. You can increase or decrease trust with each move you make.

The danger in the early stages of your leadership is that you have not earned the trust of others. You may have heard the expression the "honeymoon" period. During your leadership honeymoon, people are willing to give you the benefit of the doubt and praise your good qualities. Later on, reality will set in, and the idealized representation of you to others will be replaced by a more realistic assessment of your qualities and actions as a leader (the same process that occurs in all relationships).

When you do disappoint others, make a mistake, or alienate some employees due to a difficult decision that does not go in their favor, you may have to draw on your leadership assets to continue to lead. You need assets to lead, and these assets are earned by your actions. These assets are acquired with your acts of good will and your track record of results previously achieved. You cannot draw on your "line" authority for legitimacy and authority in your new role. It has to be earned. You earn trust and support by first getting to know people and the organization and then later by giving people what they need and adding value to the organization. This includes making effective decisions with the appropriate level of information gathering and examination of alternatives, and then taking action and doing what you say you will do.

Assuming the role of leader involves helping people understand what you have to offer and what is important to you. Leaders in transition should identify "symbolic acts" that communicate to others the important hallmarks of their leadership. You might choose to stand at the door and greet people on the opening day of a conference or workshop. This shows that you are interested in people and that you are willing to take the time to personally greet all employees. If you are a principal or superintendent, you may ride the bus on the first day of school with the students to show others that you value children and recognize the importance of the first day of school. If you are a chamber of commerce president, you may give a new business owner a "key" to the city or sit in the dunk tank during community days and get soaked to raise money for charity.

Symbolic acts are real acts of your leadership but may be carefully selected during transition to communicate a message about you and your leadership. You may sport the company logo to show people that you are now a part of the organization and proud to be an employee. Declining a reserved parking spot may show employees that you are not willing to accept a benefit that sets you apart from most employees. Even though you are different from the employees that you supervise, you may wish to diminish the obvious distinctions to earn their trust and respect. These symbolic acts must be consistent with the authentic you. *Each move you make must be consistent with your core values and be real.* What you do will say more about you than your words.

COMMUNICATION AND CREDIBILITY

Leadership is a relationship with people, and successful leaders know how to build relationships and gain the support of others. Use transition as an opportunity to open up lines of communication with internal stakeholders and external customers as well. The best way to build a relationship and earn trust is to focus on the "other" (not the "self") and listen to what they have to say. Get off the stage! Take the time to be visible and talk to as many people as you can.

Make a list of key communicators at all levels of the organization and develop a plan to meet and talk to them. Identify the key players inside the organization and the external constituents that contribute to or influence the organization's success. Key communicators and partners should be identified and a plan established to meet and communicate with valuable contacts and supporters during the early days of your tenure. Sometimes people in the organization can introduce you to others and serve as your host.

Whenever possible, meet people at their work locations rather than in your office. It may be helpful to be introduced by another employee, board member, or stakeholder. Include people who are part of your support network and enlist their help in developing an effective communication plan. Make sure that you are meeting people who can give you valuable information and support.

Regardless of the status or influence of the people you meet, make sure that you are a considerate listener. One employee told me a story about a new superintendent and his actions when he was first introduced to the community. According to the principal, the new superintendent's obvious preference for important people soon became a source of amusement to employees. He was described as a giant magnet that was highly attracted to anyone rich and powerful.

The employee said, "As soon as he would enter a room, it was like he was wearing a magnet. Someone important would be there, and it was like his feet left the ground and he lost control of his body. He would be drawn to the most important person in the room like a powerful magnet. He couldn't help himself; he felt the pull of all that money and influence." The new superintendent resigned after nine months of service for personal reasons (meaning the school board gave him a negative performance review, and his contract was not going to get renewed). Another employee commented, "He didn't want to be a leader, he wanted to be a king!"

If there is a desk between you and your visitors, get out from behind your desk and sit down next to them. Be courteous, friendly, patient, and interested in the speaker. Take responsibility for making sure they are at ease and that this is a convenient time to talk. Ask them about themselves and share something about yourself. Tell them why you are meeting with them or ask them what they would like to accomplish during the meeting. The meeting should accomplish the goals of everyone involved.

Prepare questions that are open-ended and likely to allow for a rich conversation. Let people take the conversation in a direction that suits them. The only agenda on the table should be getting to know others and finding out what you can about the organization. Give people the gift of your time and attention while being sensitive to their interests and schedule. Eventually you will find out what you need to know without making the discussion feel like an interrogation. When you really listen to others, it shows that you care about them. Good listening doesn't require agreement; it just requires that you fully understand another's message. *You can listen without committing to a course of action*. Listen to understand and appreciate others and their viewpoints.

YOUR SKILL AS A LISTENER

Listening is a skill and requires practice. Effective listeners attend to both verbal and nonverbal messages and make sure they understand the intent of the speaker. If you want to be a careful listener, then stop thinking about what you want to say next. Rephrase and summarize the ideas that were shared. Keep your body still and lean forward with a relaxed posture. Make good eye contact and let the speaker know by your body language and verbal responses that you are listening intently. Relax. Do not interrupt the speaker; focus on his or her needs and message to you.

If you are highly verbal, you may want to talk more than you want to listen. Resist the temptation. If you are a nervous conversationalist, you may allow the conversation to go on for too long or put the burden of the conversation on the other person. Build your skills as a conversationalist. Although it may never feel natural, you can improve your communication skills with practice. People will see the effort you put into the conversation and help you out.

If you initiated the discussion, it is your responsibility to signal when it is over. If you are uncomfortable with ending the conversation, ask the speaker to evaluate the conversation for you. You might say, "We'll have more time to talk in the future. Do you think I have some understanding of you and your role as an employee?" If the discussion topics are challenging and more time is needed, make arrangements to meet the individual or group again. Always thank people for their time and highlight a few things that you learned from them.

If you are serious about building relationships and gaining the support of people, you should be willing to identify your strengths and limitations as a communicator and do something about it. A frequently cited reason for the failure of leaders is poor communication. More often than not, it is your skill as a listener that is critical to your success. If you listen only to what you want to hear, then you won't learn about difficult issues or how someone else might feel, and you might miss negative feedback about your performance. This is one of the most limiting and crippling aspects of leadership: You're the last person to realize that you are failing. If that describes you, then change your course of action today or figure out how you can begin to get honest feedback without punishing the messenger.

People should feel safe to tell you what they think without fear of negative judgments or consequences. Listening requires emotional maturity and a willingness to suspend your judgment and your agenda for the sake of someone else and their ideas. It is a core ingredient needed to build healthy relationships between and among leaders and members. If your motivation to communicate with others is sincere, people

will help and support you even if you are an awkward conversationalist. If you lack sincerity, they will know it in a heartbeat. Leaders who
put in too much time at their desks will not build relationships or earn
the support of people. Push yourself out the door and spend time with
people. Effective leaders spend more time with people than on tasks,
particularly executive leaders at the top of an organization. People are
their priority, and listening is a critical communication and survival
skill.

FIFTEEN MINUTES OF FAME

When you are a new leader, other people may say and do things that
will make you feel important. You may be asked a lot of questions
about yourself and how you intend to work with others. People will
want to build a relationship with you and gain your support. You may
be introduced as someone's "new boss." You might get your nameplate
on the door or receive a box of new business cards. Watch your ego and
conduct. That you are experiencing your first fifteen minutes of fame
(and it feels good) doesn't mean you should stay on the stage. People
will be curious about you and motivated to figure out what is important
to you and how you intend to lead. You should disclose some important
information about yourself. This may include your excitement about
your new role, your appreciation for the opportunity to work with others, and the things that are important to you.

The key is balance. Don't tell your life story or go on too much about
yourself. People will not gossip about your values and ideals; they will
gossip when you give them something to talk about that is often not
flattering. Tell people things you want to read in the newspaper, and
don't engage in "trouble talk" or bragging to win others over or enlist
their support. However, if you don't disclose some things about yourself, people will believe that you are hiding something, and you will not
earn their trust. If you don't share something about yourself, people
may wonder about your motivation to lead. Be open and authentic and
share some of the healthy and positive things in your life.

Remember to start by asking others to tell you what's important to
them. If your "entrance talk" is all about you and your ideas, people
will conclude that you are focused on yourself, not on them or the or-

ganization. They'll see that you didn't take the time to get to know them and earn their trust. Figure out what you want to say, and repeat the central leadership message that you developed as one component of your entrance plan. This will keep you from talking too much and allow you the time to listen to others.

If you are a "doer," not a talker, you will still need to share some things about yourself. Look for opportunities to get to know people by attending events or volunteering. Just showing up and listening to a committee meeting is an effective strategy. If learning is important to you, then participate in professional development opportunities with employees or step in and ask people during a planned break about what they are learning and why it is important. Get involved, be yourself, and be visible—these are the keys to your success in the first stages of transition.

After you have had an opportunity to learn about your organization, discuss your observations with others and ask them to confirm whether what you are observing is correct from their point of view. Your observations will be appreciated and reveal to others that you took the time to learn about them. During transition your goal is to assume the role of leader, build relationships and gain support, and identify a future direction. If you have done your homework properly, your leadership entrance plan will help you build a solid foundation for winning support and identifying worthy goals and directions for the future. The next step is to identify the goals and future direction and develop some initial short- and long-term strategies to signal this future vision to others.

CONDUCTING AN ORGANIZATIONAL AUDIT

During the early phases of transition, you will not only meet people but gather information that helps you understand your department or organization's history and position in the field. Conducting an organizational audit involves gathering data in the following areas of history and operations:

- The organization's history (including information about the founders, heroes and heroines, critical events, and previous track record of successes, failures, or both)

- The informal and formal political and social structures in place (networks, relationships, alliances, and pressure points)
- The results of an assessment of the methods to accomplish the primary work and the current levels of performance, productivity, or achievement (quality standards, rate of production/success, profit/loss, goal attainment, etc.)
- The results of an analysis of the stage of your department, school, or organization's life cycle (growing or declining—in a start-up mode, continuously improving, bankrupt, or corrupt?)
- The results of a comparative analysis of your product or service as benchmarked by standards or competitors (issues of quality and competition)
- A list of the key organizational concerns, challenges, and opportunities

This process gives you the raw data to identify and set the stage for the future direction. This process can and should involve others. The organizational audit produces a set of assumptions about the current status of the organization and highlights some potential directions for change. These preliminary findings are organized and shared with as wide an audience as needed to assess their validity and to gain consensus on the critical issues for the future.

LEVERAGE OPPORTUNITIES

A leverage opportunity is an action-oriented strategy to overcome resistance and propel people to accomplish more with greater speed by using an event, factor, or condition as a lever to spur action. A crisis can serve as a lever to propel people and the organization forward, inspire commitment, open up new ways of thinking creatively, and inspire higher levels of cooperation and collaboration. Change rarely happens unless something appears in the environment that impacts people and their assessment of their future stability and success. Changes in leadership can be leverage opportunities if the advantage is mined and the assessment of the current reality is accurate and challenging to the long-term survival of people and the organization.

If declining sales, fewer customers, poor student achievement, a reduction in government support, or other conditions don't favor the future of an organization, these conditions or factors can spur action and become a lever for change. It takes a leader, or leadership, to see them as an opportunity and to capitalize on them with creative solutions and energy. Sharing the data with a wide audience and asking for the leverage points will help you and others figure out how to engage in strategic action. The goals are people, quality, and the long-term survival of the organization.

It is enough just to complete an organizational auditing process during the period of transition (the first six months). *An organizational audit is a review of practices, systems, and performance data to identify the strengths and current capacity of your department, school, or organization.* This process is a lot like the preliminary process of strategic planning. Data are examined, trends are identified, programs and practices are reviewed, and the challenges for the future are explored. This is a creative enterprise that involves a great deal of study and discernment.

The next stage of this process is to draw conclusions from the data, explore alternatives, and identify what areas are critical to explore, exploit, or address. Using a strength-based approach, the strategic leader figures out how talents and strengths can be used to optimize the current performance or set the stage for future growth. The organizational audit helps to identify the gap between the current and desired level of achievement. Once key issues or findings emerge from this process, the next step is to find ways that others can be made aware of this information and participate in the reinvention of themselves and the organization.

Strategic leaders know how to select the winning idea or direction that not only will move the organization forward but will set the stage for the possibility of renewal and transformation. The leader asks, what new direction can result in ensuring the long-term success and viability of the department, school, or organization? This direction can be identified by the leader or through a consensus or collaboration model with group ownership and involvement. The factors associated with how this decision is reached and how the support of others is gained are contextual and based on employees, the current state of the organization, the culture, and the external environment. After identifying significant trends and developing a set of preliminary ideas for action, the leader seeks support for the new direction.

You can gain the understanding and support of employees for the future direction by discussing the challenges of change with them, sharing the results of an organizational audit, and asking them for their ideas. You have set the stage for this discussion because you have communicated the important hallmarks of your leadership and you took the time to talk to people and learn about the organization and its past. During the early stages of your tenure as leader you can build ownership and consensus for the future direction by identifying winning goals that will serve people and the organization well over the longterm. The goals of transition are met when the future direction is securely established and a plan of action to support this new direction is devised. Once this plan is firmly in place, the next step is to enlist the support of others in accomplishing the goals, whether they involve incremental improvement or transformational change.

RENEWAL AND COMMITMENT

The transition phase includes preparing for the future leadership role and identifying issues within the organization that will have a bearing on the future leader's successful transition into the new role. It is also a time to examine issues that challenge the organization and strategically use the transition phases to renew energy and commitment to achieving the goals of the organization. The seeds for building an effective direction are planted during the transition and provide a vehicle for enlisting the support of employees toward the accomplishment of goals.

During times of considerable challenge and change, it is especially critical that people renew their commitment to work together as a team and emphasize collaboration over competition. Make sure that the informal leaders in an organization are identified and included in strategy sessions and decision-making processes. This measure provides reassurance to the rank and file employees who are symbolically represented by highly valued colleagues. As a new leader, you need to ask others to help you establish a new direction and to give you an opportunity to earn their support. This happens when you identify worthy goals as a result of an *inclusive* and *defensible* process. If the plan and the process are sound, people will support you. Remember that leaders earn the temporary permission of members to lead, and this permission is based on the leader's credibility, assessment of employees' needs and goals, and past record for meeting those needs. If you have let others see the authentic you and demonstrated your qualities as an effective leader during transition, others will support you.

CHAPTER 9

Leaders and Crisis Management

A PLAYGROUND SHOOTING

On a beautiful fall day in Sheridan, Wyoming, an intruder appeared on a middle-school playground and within seconds began to randomly discharge his gun into the midst of the students. Although some students were injured, no one died. Before he could be stopped, the shooter committed suicide in front of the students. This horror-filled event took place in plain view of many classrooms.

Emergency-management personnel responded quickly to the call for help and took charge of the injured students. They quickly contained the crisis and sealed off the area where the assailant had taken his life. The responsibility of school leaders was to manage the responses of parents and students who reacted to the crisis in predictable ways.

Hysterical parents panicked and rushed to the school site to pull their children out of school. Over 600 cars converged on the school within minutes of the crisis. Because there was no place to park, parents simply left their cars in the street. Phones were jammed, streets were closed, and chaos reigned outside the school. The shooting became a nationwide media event, and soon the press converged at the school site as well.

The school officials remained calm and instituted a checkout system designed for the orderly dismissal of students. Counselors were immediately available to students, families, and employees. Communication officers and the superintendent worked with the media. School officials contacted emotionally fragile students to reduce the risk of an overreaction to the tragedy and harm to themselves. Decisions were made about how to reopen school and how to identify the psychological needs of students and parents at reentry to the school site. The first few weeks were difficult, but eventually the school and the school system returned to a state of stability.

This is a true story of the 1992 playground shooting in Sheridan, Wyoming, and was related to me by Dr. Craig Beck, then assistant principal of Sheridan High School and a member of the school-crisis-management team that responded to the crisis. Although the appearance of a shooter on a playground is difficult to predict, it is not difficult to anticipate the increasing amount of violence in our society and its potential dangers. This situation and, unfortunately, many others like it fit the definition of a crisis.

CRISIS MANAGEMENT

A crisis is any situation or event that poses a significant threat of loss of life, property, or other assets and that may potentially impact the long-term vitality and stability of an individual, family, organization, or community. Both natural and human-made crises may cause a loss of life and property. The loss of property can be easily identified and quantified. For example, property damage is assessed based on the cost of replacement. Some crises create conditions in which assets are lost that are difficult to measure. For instance, it is of course impossible to place a value on lost life. At the same time, scandal involving the waste of tax dollars on expensive travel by legislators can create a crisis for the elected leader and cause a loss of the leader's reputational assets. These "soft" assets may be difficult to quantify but are valuable to the survival of people and the organization. They may include (1) the reputation of the organization and its personnel, (2) anticipated future revenues, (3) the quality of leadership, or (4) the organization's capacity to respond to change.

The difference between a tragedy and a crisis is that a tragedy injures people, property, or assets and causes damage, while a crisis threatens survival. Each type of crisis has some common elements (the causes of the crisis and the way it progresses before order is restored) and some unique elements (the signs that warn of a potential threat and the actions required to deescalate the crisis event). A natural disaster requires emergency management, while a preventable crisis involves crisis management.[1] This chapter outlines the expectations and actions of leaders related to human-made, preventable crises.

General knowledge of crisis management prepares leaders to respond effectively to a crisis event. Knowledge of specific types of crises can result in a more focused and rapid response. The discovery of unethical insider trading causes a legal, financial, and reputational crisis that is predictable. A terrorist attack creates multiple crises associated with loss of life, property, and confidence in the economic and governmental system. Some acts, like the terrorist attacks of 9-11-01, can be imagined but not predicted with certainty. The discipline of crisis management requires leaders to imagine the unimaginable and then prepare for it.

Individuals, families, organizations, and communities are expected to protect themselves from the potential damage of a crisis by adopting preventative-management strategies to ward off any potential threat. Knowledge about each type of crisis results in more successful efforts to contain the crisis early, minimize damage, and restore order.[2] During times of crisis, people look for leadership and expect leaders to take action.

Leaders, particularly senior executives, governmental officials, or school superintendents and principals, need to know the potential causes of various crises, establish procedures to prevent them, and minimize the damage of any crisis event as quickly as possible. This expectation is also true of middle management and all employees to a lesser degree. Even though you may not be directly responsible for a preventable crisis, leaders are held accountable for the results of the crisis if it is mismanaged or the damage sustained is excessive.

LEADING PEOPLE AND MANAGING THE CRISIS

Effective leaders must successfully face two challenges in crisis management by (1) managing the crisis itself (and all the multiple crises that may follow) and (2) leading the people and the organization affected by the crisis until order is restored. There is a delicate balance between meeting the operational challenge of the crisis and attending to the human needs. For example, if lives are to be saved, a crisis may require immediate and sophisticated rescue operations, and they may be very risky. The other duty of leaders is to attend to the needs of people, showing empathy and communicating frequently with accurate information. Leaders attend funerals, comfort families, request resources, and maintain a physical presence with people during the crisis. It is dangerous to fail in either area—managing the crisis or attending to the human needs.

There are four common stages or phases of crisis management: (1) prevention and preparation, (2) reaction and containment, (3) stabilization and postcrisis learning, and (4) innovation and renewal. Action-oriented leaders must simultaneously address the challenges associated with crisis management by understanding the actions during each phase of crisis management and the role of leaders during a crisis.

PHASE 1: PREVENTION AND PREPARATION

Fires in Yellowstone National Park have threatened lives and property in the Jackson Hole, Wyoming, area several times over the last 100 years. Natural disasters are not preventable. A bolt of lightning ignites a tree, and strong winds can quickly cause a burning tree to become a raging fire. Natural disasters require emergency response preparedness and fast action at the onset of a crisis.

The cause and type of crisis affect the cycle of response. If the cause is natural, the response is to save lives, contain the damage, and take care of the survivors. However, if careless forest management causes the fire (some "controlled burns" by the Forest Service become uncontrollable fires), then it becomes a human-made crisis and requires both crisis and emergency-management procedures. When the crisis is preventable, leaders are expected to go beyond the immediate management of the crisis and take steps to ensure that the crisis does not happen again.[3]

Leaders often describe the process of crisis management as "putting out a fire before the place burns down." The discipline of crisis management is much like the practice of fighting fires. Like effective fire fighting, a large part of effective crisis management is preparing for the possibility of a fire. Knowledge about effective practices for specific types of crises is available to students of crisis management. Most leaders do not want anything to happen "on their watch," and the threat of a crisis requires knowledge, preparation, vigilance, and fast action.

During the prevention stage of crisis management, the leadership team anticipates the possibility of various types of crises and employs improvement strategies to ward off or minimize the damage if a crisis occurs. The theory of crisis management is that crises caused by people are preventable. Planning activities and the early detection of a potential crisis are very effective in minimizing or controlling the threat and the resulting damage. The process of prevention requires a review of all the systems associated with the health and vitality of an organization.

The purpose of a review of systems is to uncover areas of vulnerability and employ preventative maintenance or improve strategies to protect the vital assets. This may involve the proper care and maintenance of capital equipment or ensuring that operating procedures are followed to provide for the safety of people and property. If areas are found to be vulnerable to crises, changes in process or practices are required.

Prevention involves planning and imagination. Using a systems approach, all areas of the organization are reviewed, and a crisis-management team examines critical areas of concern. *A systems approach is defined as a holistic and thorough examination of every area of operation and the relationship between and among these various areas of operation to determine the potential impact if a change or crisis occurs.* For example, if a production line is temporarily halted, what other areas of operation are affected? How does a reduction in student enrollment impact personnel or capital-improvement projects? What happens when there is an increase or decrease in the sales department? What happens when the information network collapses?

Most executives and school administrators are very concerned with student and employee safety. The definition of safety has expanded to include physical and psychological safety (including appropriate accommodation for disabilities and freedom from harassment and health-related injuries affecting the employees' personal and work life). While many school leaders understand emergency routines for natural disasters, they may be unprepared for new threats, including random acts of vio-lence, intruders at the school site, student-to-student harassment, or the spread of disease. Leaders may be very aware of safety needs but may be unprepared for the disruption of business, a loss of the public trust, or product tampering that causes injury or death. Knowledge of the early detection and identification of a crisis is critical to the success of the leader and the organization.

Detecting Areas of Vulnerability

The challenge to leadership is to assess the likelihood of the threat, the process for gaining support for the preventative strategy, and the costs in human and capital resources to improve each area of operation. Some preventative measures are effective yet would not be tolerated. For example, controlled access to a public area may not be realistic or tolerated unless the threat is viewed as realistic and imminent. Mem-bers of a crisis-management or leadership team determine what course of action is prudent and attainable within the resources that are avail-able and the political reality.

If the threat is underestimated and significant damage occurs, the re-sult can be disastrous for the survivors, the leader(s), the employees, and the organization. However, an excessive amount of resources spent on prevention takes resources away from other critical areas vital to the organization (research and development activities, employee compen-sation, professional development, and the like). Areas that are poorly funded, yet vital to the organization, may become a new threat to the organization's long-term stability.

Prevention and preparation are linked together to ensure a successful crisis-management strategy. You prevent a crisis by anticipating it and eliminating areas of vulnerability. You prepare for a crisis (in the event it occurs despite your preventative strategies) by anticipating the nature of the crisis as it unfolds and planning your response(s) to the crisis event. Plans for responding to each type of crisis are developed by ask-ing what-if questions. If your preventative strategies are effective, a team will detect the early signals of a crisis and take corrective action to prevent or contain it.

For each type of crisis, the team looks for signs or signals of an emerging crisis and identifies potential actions and reactions to various scenarios.[4] A list of potential actions and reactions for each stage of the crisis is developed. Key personnel are listed and resources identified. Practice exercises such as using case studies to learn from the experience of others, simulating experiences, and debriefing after a practice or real crisis event increase the knowledge and readiness of the team. The first line of defense against a potential crisis is assessing the nature of the threat as it appears in the environment.

During the prevention and preparation stages, a leader should do the following to establish and develop an effective crisis-management team:

- Acquire knowledge and develop technical expertise about the management of various types of crises
- Examine the effectiveness of various systems (human and physical) and identify potential threats and preventative strategies
- Identify the conditions that are potentially hazardous and establish systems to detect the signals of a crisis as early as possible
- Participate in continuous training activities to ensure rapid response to a crisis and coordinate efforts with other agencies
- Maintain equipment, use technology, and acquire resources to react quickly to a crisis event
- Maintain vigilance and preparedness for the future

PHASE 2: REACTION AND CONTAINMENT

The second phase of crisis management is reaction and containment. The goal during the reaction phase is to correctly assess the nature of a problem as a potential threat and to react to it with the appropriate level of resources and energy. Reacting too early to a potential threat can create a crisis out of what otherwise might be a nonevent. Reacting too late to a crisis can result in dire consequences. During the reaction phase, the challenge is to detect the early signs of trouble and provide the appropriate direction, energy, and resources to address the threat.

Early Warning Signs

The signs or signals of a crisis are the early warning signs that something is amiss in the environment. Signs of financial mismanagement might be frequent requests for the transfer of funds from one budget category to another or the failure to provide accurate and timely information on the status of the budget. Signs of a threat to safety might be the accumulation of combustible materials without proper disposal or the increasing frequency of accidents at a work site. The threat of violence might be prevented if unusual and threatening behaviors are identified and assistance in dealing with the problem and protecting others is arranged.

The Enron financial scandal of 2002 followed early signals of irregularities in auditing practices. The alleged irregularities were reported by Sherron Watkins, an Enron vice president for corporate development and former employee of Arthur Andersen. Watkins notified Enron chairman Kenneth Lay that she suspected that irregularities and potentially illegal auditing practices had allowed Enron to hide its losses and misrepresent its financial condition. Enron corporate officers and board members allegedly ignored these concerns and continued to misrepresent the company's true financial conditions to the public. Later Andrew Fastow, Enron's chief financial officer, was arrested on charges of fraud and conspiracy to commit fraud.

Watkins also reported her concerns to her former employer, the auditing firm of Arthur Andersen. The response of Arthur Andersen to the emerging crisis was allegedly to shred documents. Finally, Enron acknowledged the unreported losses after the government launched an investigation into the irregularities. Bankruptcy was later declared, and investigations of the causes are still underway at the time of this writing. Unfortunately, scandals in more corporations followed.

The public uproar over this deception led to (1) the dismissal of executives, (2) bankruptcy, (3) financial loss to investors and employees, (4) reputational damage to people and organizations related to the crisis, and (5) public rage over the lack of checks and balances in the system to prevent this crisis from occurring. This crisis has created multiple crises that will take years to address. Why are some early warning signs and problems ignored?

Faced with the possibility of a crisis, some individuals and organizations may choose to ignore the threat rather than acknowledge it and devote the time and energy needed to address the situation. Although there were rumors in the investment community regarding the uncertain financial performance of Enron, no one wanted Enron to fail—not the board members, executives, employees, stockholders, investment counselors, or government regulators. A failure meant that stock would fall in value, corporate officers would suffer a loss of reputation and perhaps face civil or criminal suits, and a significant energy provider would be in danger of going out of business.

Even elected officials who benefited from large campaign contributions were indirectly involved in the crisis. Politicians did not want to be associated with corporate officers involved in the scandal. They had a stake in avoiding the reputational damage that could occur if the media or public believed that Enron bought influence through its campaign contributions. If the public perceived that influence had been purchased in the form of campaign contributions, there would be many changes in leadership after the elections.

Signs of trouble may be ignored if the environment is full of crises, and this is just one among many fires to extinguish. When a crisis appears imminent, it might be ignored because acknowledging the crisis can have dire negative consequences and the action that brought it on can't be changed. Sometimes success can breed failure. People and organizations that have a solid track record of success may become victims of their own success. Success may cause complacency; commitment of the time and effort necessary to monitor potential problems or threats might be replaced by an attitude of invincibility. Sometimes there just isn't enough money to plug all of the holes of vulnerability. The resources needed to seriously combat the crisis are nonexistent. When a problem or threat is ignored or undetected and early intervention does not take place, a full-blown crisis can occur. Crisis management must now shift into reaction and containment. The goal is to save lives, property, and assets and to contain the crisis.

Reaction and containment are the most challenging phases of crisis management because, once the threat is recognized, the management of the crisis requires rapid processing of incomplete information, decisiveness, courage, and immediate action. Taking command of a situation means having the courage to lead. People expect leaders to be prepared for a crisis and to make the right decisions under very stressful circumstances.

While emergency-management personnel are highly experienced in disaster management, school administrators, public officials, and corporate executives engage in crisis management on a nonroutine basis. The challenge for school and business leaders is to learn how to manage a crisis once it begins. Learning how to cooperate with emergency-management personnel is only one part of crisis management. Effective leaders know they have a role in the crisis and never give up the responsibility for contributing to the successful management of the overall crisis even if emergency-management personnel take charge of some aspects of the crisis.

Taking responsibility for communication, leaders work with employees, media, and community members to lead people through a crisis. They continuously communicate with the community of people connected to the event and do whatever it takes to direct or support the containment of the crisis. Whether you are a superintendent of schools, a mayor, or a chief executive officer, when there is an explosion, an attack against people, or a work-related injury, you need to communicate and take some responsibility for managing the crisis. This is true even if emergency-management personnel are addressing the immediate threat.

While the crisis event is happening, leaders address the demands of the employees and the public for information about how and why the crisis occurred in the first place. The most frequently asked question is, what caused this crisis and who is responsible? It is important to provide accurate information and to fully disclose what you can. It is a mistake to guess at the facts or the causes and potential consequences of the crisis. Describe the facts of the crisis and tell what is being done to respond to it and prevent any further damage.

Perhaps the single most important ingredient of leading people is optimism. Regardless of their inner doubts or concerns, leaders must maintain optimism that recovery is possible and that the outlook for the future is positive. This is critical to the emotional health of survivors. Many executives on September 11, 2001, said that although they had doubts about their corporations' surviving, they maintained optimism and demonstrated creativity in fighting for their survival.

This optimism made a tremendous difference in managing the crisis and the results.

During the reaction and containment phase, leaders should do the following:

- Implement a process and obtain resources to restore order beginning with rescue and recovery efforts of people and property (human lives and safety are number one)
- Establish a chain of command for decision making and a "chain of process" for managing the various stages of the crisis
- Communicate about the crisis and provide accurate and timely information while remaining calm
- Identify resources and coordinate efforts
- Communicate about the cause(s) of the crisis (how it happened and who is responsible) and provide facts and figures about the damage sustained
- Frame the crisis for the members by describing the nature of the crisis and share information about how this type of crisis develops and is managed
- Offer reassurance and support to survivors, including their need to move through the stages of grieving toward acceptance
- Stay with the crisis during the initial stages of crisis management until order is restored, overseeing the operations associated with rescue and recovery efforts
- Provide moral support to rescue workers and participate in some of the rescue work
- Inspire and mobilize people to contribute during the various phases of the crisis
- Communicate a sense of optimism about the future and take steps to support the morale of the survivors during the various stages of grieving

PHASE 3: STABILIZATION AND POSTCRISIS LEARNING

Once the immediate threat is over, either the emergency-response personnel hand back the crisis to the leaders and organization or the initial responses to the threat have taken their course (the crisis event has unfolded and is widely known). It may be that after the initial crisis, multiple crises follow (for example, financial collapse, changes in leadership, or civil or criminal charges). These must also be managed. The nature of the crisis event determines the course of action needed to move through it.

When the crisis is significant, more time is needed to address its complex and multiple challenges. Once the initial containment phase has occurred, the next phase of crisis management takes place. The process of stabilization and postcrisis learning occurs shortly after the crisis event occurs. This phase begins when it is possible to return to some normal or temporary routines and there is an opportunity to learn from the crisis events. *Stabilization is a process of returning to the routine functions of the organization once the conditions that led to the crisis are successfully contained and order and safety are secured.*

If there was a loss of life, a memorial service is planned and resources are provided to families. If a facility has been closed, it is cleaned, inspected, and secured. Information on all aspects of the crisis is provided to returning employees, parents, students, or community members. Although the crisis continues to require management, the focus is on the affective or human needs of people impacted by the crisis, the operational issues associated with the crisis event, or both. The goal of stabilization is to return to a predictable environment that is safe and not subject to the same threats presented by the initial crisis.

Postcrisis learning involves a systematic review of the crisis event with the goal of eliminating conditions that can lead to a future crisis and improving performance during the management of the crisis. A formal, systematic review is a complete investigation of the crisis. A case study or formal report is written that describes the crisis in detail. Experts or participants with first-hand knowledge or experience in the crisis event are interviewed. Data is collected and events are described in chronological order. A complete and accurate report of the crisis is written, much like an investigative report.

The next step is to read the report and share it with a crisis-management team (consisting of employees from all departments and ranks) and the executive team. Debriefing meetings are held to discuss the information and ideas about the cause(s) and systemwide impact. The focus is on the crisis event and all the related systems. Performance during all phases of the crisis is examined and evaluated using the goals of the crisis-intervention process. Questions are asked, such as, was communication effective and did the right information get to the right people? All areas are reviewed, and recommendations for further investigation or improvements are summarized.

Postcrisis learning is a significant asset if the knowledge of people involved in the crisis is used to plan for the future. Even a simple postcrisis debriefing of key players about the performance of people and systems and an examination of areas for improvement can be very effective. The postcrisis debriefing should be conducted in the spirit of investigation rather than finger-pointing. Recommendations for future improvements are part of the next phase of crisis management—innovation and renewal.

Leaders should do the following during stabilization and postcrisis learning:

- Identify the affective or human needs of people associated with the crisis and devise an aftercare plan for the survivors
- Make improvements or changes to the facility or "location" of the crisis event (if one exists) to ensure that the conditions that led to the threat are eliminated to the degree possible. If the location of the crisis is the administrative headquarters, identify some areas where the "cleanup" is visible (change in leader, policy, direction, etc.)
- Make changes in policy, procedures, role expectations, or all three, to increase vigilance and improve the systems that contributed or led to the breakdown in systems or acceleration of the crisis event
- Conduct a postcrisis investigation and identify all the facts related to the crisis event; develop a formal report
- Organize a team of employees or community members to scrutinize the report and make recommendations
- Communicate about the crisis event, the steps that were taken, and the lessons that were learned. Reach all people associated with the crisis event

- Share the results of the formal study with the crisis-management team and senior leadership team, the board of directors, all employees and stakeholders, and the public as appropriate
- Devise a plan to follow up on the recommendations and ensure the needed changes have been made

PHASE 4: INNOVATION AND RENEWAL

A crisis is an event and also a turning point in the lives of individuals, families, organizations, or communities. Things can never go back to being the way they were. The psychological costs are uncertainty and insecurity. The result is a temporary loss of productivity and optimism. When crisis occurs, it always creates change. Since a crisis event is a threat to survival, it often results in a substantial change in perspective, practice, performance, or plans. The presence of so many interrelated systems means that a crisis tends to have a ripple effect that sends out shockwaves beyond the immediate crisis event. The productive response to crisis is innovation and renewal. These are the two useful weapons to combat the damage of a crisis event. Innovation and renewal cannot occur until the survivors have been allowed to grieve and the process of stabilization has occurred. Expecting people to make dramatic changes on the tail of a major crisis is unrealistic and doomed to fail. The goal of stabilization is to restore order (to the degree possible) and to increase survivor productivity and security.

Innovation is possible during the crisis (to contain it and restore order) or after the stabilization and postcrisis learning phase occurs (to make sure that neither this nor anything else ever threatens us again). Effective leaders know that a threat is also an opportunity in which new levels of flexibility, openness, and support for innovative ideas are possible. The crisis event causes a breakdown in the walls between people and creates a period of unusual collaboration. Suddenly, the crisis is the enemy and everyone is impacted by it. The threat to survival can motivate people to develop improved and innovative systems to fix the problem and go beyond the immediate crisis.

The psychological impact of surviving a crisis can create unity, cooperation, and determination. People collaborate across levels and share resources, understand how various systems work and relate to each other, and override bureaucratic rules and procedures to react quickly to the crisis event. I recall seeing a sign that read "trust = speed." The trust created from a survival event can generate better relationships and speed up the normally slow process of change. Changes that might have required a significant approval process are implemented at lightning speed if the change has the potential to reduce the threat or contain the crisis. *An innovation is defined as a change in thinking, action, or both that impacts people, perspectives, processes, and production.* Innovation causes renewal. *Renewal is defined as the systemic reinvention of a living system (individuals, families, organizations, communities) accomplished by retaining things of value, discarding outdated ideas or methods, and inventing new strategies to ensure future survival.*

If the response to the crisis is productive, the crisis culminates in renewal. Of course, the best defense against a crisis is to minimize the hazards of human error and develop strategies for systemic improvement. The idea is to leverage the knowledge of systems to create a learning organization that is continuously improving. Crisis management assumes that crisis is preventable and that even when crises do occur, they can be contained, and learning occurs as a result of it. Leaders must prepare for crisis management by understanding what conditions contribute to the likelihood of a crisis and then by systematically addressing each threat with a preventative strategy.

When under fire, leaders must accept the responsibility for others and move through the phases of crisis management with knowledge and strategic thinking. Finally, leaders must understand that mistakes will be made (by themselves and others) and prepare themselves for the challenges and responsibilities of leadership. During the innovation and renewal phase, leaders should do the following:

1. Turn the crisis into an opportunity by listening and supporting innovative ideas from the employees or participants involved
2. Understand that although a crisis threatens safety, it also motivates people to work together in ways that can create a climate of innovation (the walls are down and the environment should be "risk" free)

3. Introduce changes after people have moved through the stages of stabilization and postcrisis learning (allowing time for grieving and restoration of order)
4. Capitalize on postcrisis learning to improve and change
5. Develop a self-renewing organization that retains things of value, discards outdated ideas or methods that no longer work, and invents new strategies to ensure future survival

Although the information about crisis management applies to reputational crises, this is such a troubling and growing area of concern that I decided to address the unique dimensions of this type of crisis in a separate section.

REPUTATIONAL CRISES

In some cases, crises are ignored because executives may not want to face the consequences of identifying the concern or accept the potential disruption or consequences to the organization. Instead, attempts are made to contain or deny a threat before it becomes a crisis or to divert attention from it. These avoidance tactics may stall the damage in the short term but can cause greater damage for the executive and organization in the long run when the public learns of the deception. Any attempt to distort the truth or cover up poor performance or illegal practice will lead to a reputational crisis when discovered.

A reputational crisis occurs when the leader or the organization fails to meet the expectations for average performance or when the personal or professional actions of people connected to the organization (leaders, employees, or board members) are contrary to professional and ethical standards. Failure to tell the truth or take responsibility for the damage is usually the worst mistake. If there is wrongdoing or mismanagement involved in a crisis, it is wise to seek legal advice and be prepared to disclose and take responsibility for your role or the organization's role in the crisis.

One of the worst mistakes that leaders and organizations can make is to deny any responsibility for a human-made crisis. Denying responsibility, shifting the blame, understating the problem, or describing yourself as a victim of the problem are all tactics used by people in trouble to avoid taking responsibility for their actions (or nonactions).

AVOIDANCE TACTICS

The goal of avoidance is to delay a response or shift the blame to other individuals or circumstances. Think of some examples of avoidance that you have observed. Here are some strategies that people and organizations involved in crises use to avoid facing the crisis event:

- *It's not a problem!* The leader ignores the existence of a threat by denying its existence, questioning the facts, challenging the process used to get the information, deceiving others by restating the facts, or downplaying the potential impact of the problem.
- *It's not my fault!* The leader reduces or spreads the responsibility for the crisis by finding a scapegoat to take the blame or expanding the number of people potentially responsible for the threat.
- *I'm a victim too!* The leader portrays him- or herself as a victim of the crisis (my reputation and family have been damaged by this) and offers alternative justifications and explanations for conduct.
- *I was just too busy!* The leader shifts the blame to the demands of the job or claims other interests or priorities take away from the threat or crisis area.
- *I had poor advice (my lawyer made me do it)!* The leader fails to take the time to learn enough about the problem and relies on experts for advice (and that advice was wrong or illegal).
- *Me first!* The leader makes sure that his or her career and safety are assured and tries to avoid a loss of support and reputation as a result of a crisis. The leader also tries to avoid civil or criminal culpability for crisis (dereliction of duty or illegal actions).
- *It's a systems problem!* The leader avoids responsibility for his or her actions by spreading the decision and consequences across the executive team and the entire organization.
- *It was out of the blue!* The leader alleges that no one could have known or prepared for this type of crisis. (This is a failure of the prevention and planning phase.)

- *Hey*, *it's legal!* The leader alleges that the actions skirted the edge of the law and were legal, thus asserting that there was no wrongdoing despite the obvious damage that occurred.

It is important to take charge of the crisis and to take responsibility. Do you recognize any of these avoidance tactics? Try to think about incidents of reputational crisis and how "leaders" found themselves in a hole. President Clinton denied that he had an affair with an intern and came up with his own definition of "sexual relations." The cover-up of the affair was the most damaging aspect of his presidency. Enron CEO Kenneth Lay initially stated that the company had used only legal (yet very deceptive) means to hide losses. Excessive bonuses paid to corporate officers just days before declaring bankruptcy is an example of the "me first!" tactic. Representative Gary Condit failed to fully disclose his involvement with a female intern and later appeared in an interview with Barbara Walters, portraying himself as a victim of the crisis. The interview was a colossal failure.

Ford Motor Company ignored reports of accidents related to defective tires and later tried to pass all of the blame on to Firestone tires (without accepting responsibility for its own knowledge of the problem). Eventually, Ford acknowledged the problem, recalled the defective tires, suffered financial penalties, and sustained damage to the reputation of the company and its officers. Finally, Philip Morris denied the dangers of tobacco to the body and later failed to disclose damaging facts related to its detrimental effects on the public health. It lost corporate credibility and paid enormous settlements to many states.

These cases were worthy of national media attention and may seem unrelated to small businesses, school districts, or public service agencies. However, the same problems and avoidance tactics can appear on a smaller scale. If public employees take a trip to New Orleans for a conference when there has been a reduction of employees or programs, a reputational crisis can occur. A nonprofit hospital CEO who wines and dines potential customers may feel the public's rage when these actions look unethical and a stretch of the law related to nonprofits and entertainment expenses.

It doesn't matter whether you are a public, nonprofit, or for-profit concern, the expectations and standards for professionals' personal conduct and ethical practice are the same. Reputational crises typically occur due to human error, poor judgment, or inappropriate practices. Take the time to look for any areas in your current practice that may be risky due to these factors. Your actions must pass the scrutiny of your own values and generally accepted standards for conduct and practice.

THE ENVELOPE PLEASE!

There's an old story about a new superintendent on her first day on the job. Sitting down at her desk, she opens up the center drawer and finds three sealed envelopes. The envelopes are from the departing superintendent, who has marked each envelope with a number and the following instructions: "Congratulations on your new position. When you are in serious trouble and you need some help, open the first envelope and you will find the solution to your problem." Sometime after the "honeymoon" period, the new superintendent makes her first mistake. The envelope is opened, and she reads, "Blame your predecessor." The superintendent sighs with relief, adopts the solution, and things return to normal.

Some time later, the superintendent finds herself in trouble again. Although she is reluctant to pull the second envelope out of the desk drawer, she is losing the support of the Board of Education. The message on the second envelope is brief and brilliant. It says, "Reorganize!" Once again, the superintendent implements the solution and regains the support of board members. There's only one envelope left.

A little worried about the adage "three strikes and you're out," the superintendent tucks the third envelope in the back corner of the drawer until the following year, when a third crisis arises. There's only one thing left to do. Digging into the drawer, the superintendent reluctantly tears open the third envelope, and the final solution is presented. It reads, "Prepare three envelopes!" By the time you are opening up your third envelope, your career may be on fire.

YOUR EXIT PLAN

The difference between a strategic move in your career and an emergency exit is time. The time to develop your emergency exit plan is long before the first sign of smoke. The first step in creating your emergency exit plan is to plan your escape route before you have to leave. You can do this by locating all of the exits and increasing your career fitness for your survival. If you can't dampen the flames or protect yourself from the fire that may start at any moment, you may have to implement your emergency exit plan. Your exit plan is like buying insurance — you don't need it unless there's a crisis.

Leadership does require that you take on greater career risks; it's an occupational hazard. If your career has more risk, periodically assess your chances of success. Remember Smokey the Bear? Where there's smoke, there's fire. Predictable problems in organizations lead to the demise of leaders. Poor performance in the bottom-line measures of organizational success, errors in judgment related to health and safety, change or lack of change, or events that have a devastating effect on the organization can cause your career to burn swiftly out of control.

A common leadership mistake is to ignore the potential fire hazard until it is too late. Install some smoke detectors and determine how you can get information about the safety, health, and status of your organization. If there are some smoldering issues, be the first one to identify problems and enlist the help of others in resolving them. When you've done the right thing, you've done your best work, and your career is still in flames, you may need to activate your own emergency exit plan.

The same rules for preventing a fire or fleeing a burning building apply to your career. You practiced emergency fire drills in school. Do you remember the safety rules for leaving a burning building? Stay low to the ground, cover your mouth with a damp cloth, and move swiftly! Here's a list of things you can do to plan your exit beforehand.

YOUR CAREER FITNESS CHECKLIST

1. Study your career track record, including your career moves and highlights. Ask yourself this question: would my organization hire me for this position at this rate of pay if the decision had to be made today? If the answer is no, start thinking about how to make it yes, and set some new goals.

2. Conduct a realistic assessment of your opportunities to move within your field or change careers in the near future. If the future doesn't look promising, change now. Investigate the possibilities, update your education, and learn new skills.

3. Update your resume every six months and be prepared to e-mail it to potential employers at a moment's notice.

4. Yearly, at the time of your performance appraisal, request letters of reference that attest to your success in your current position.

5. Make a list of twenty-five regular contacts in your field of work. If you haven't talked to them in the last six months, take them off your list.

6. Keep a record of continuing professional developments in your field of work. Identify the steps you have taken to continue to add value to your organization.

7. Build a portfolio of your best work that illustrates your strengths and unique talents. If the examples are electronically stored, they can be e-mailed with your resume. Make sure your work samples do not contain proprietary work owned by your company.

8. Make a list of professional contacts in career placement and continue to talk to them about career opportunities. They must know who you are and why you are someone they may want to contact in the future.

9. Read the classified employment advertisements, surf the career Web sites, and talk to others about the selection and placement practices in the marketplace. Don't wait to find this information after you have lost your job.

10. If you find yourself out of a job, don't take time off to recover. Every day you are unemployed gets harder to explain. If an opportunity is presented that meets most of your criteria, take it. Waiting too long is the same as not leaving a burning building. Get going.

11. Avoid emergency exits and figure out how you created or added fuel to the fire. If you are in a leadership role, you have to remember that things may not be rational or in your control. Be honest with yourself about what you did contribute to the

problem and learn from it. Move on to your new life by focusing on your future survival, not on your loss.

Often the role expectations for leaders are unrealistic and risky. Unrealistic as it may be, leaders are expected to stop a crisis before it begins. Not all factors that led to a crisis are under the control of leaders. However, the management of the crisis is the responsibility of leadership. A crisis can bring on unprecedented change that can be either productive or destructive. Learning to think strategically and understanding the hazards and traps associated with poor decision making are vital to the success of leaders and the organization.

A crisis, if managed poorly, can create a series of crises that threaten survival. A crisis, if managed effectively, can limit the damage of the potential threat or real loss. It can motivate people to innovate and improve and restore the organization to a more desired state after the crisis has been contained. A period of stability allows an organization to focus on the long-term development of people and the capacity of the organization. Capable organizations ensure that there is organizational flexibility and creativity during competitive times and the ability and will to survive during times of crisis.

YOUR EXIT CARD

Leadership is a choice. If you were not in your current position, what would you be doing?[5] Write your answer on a blank card. What three conditions would influence you to leave your current position? Add those conditions to your card. Your exit or courage card is an expression of the values you hold dear and your bottom line. It alerts you to the conditions that would cause you to make a change in your life.

I interviewed twenty-six female superintendents about the ethical challenges they faced in their role as superintendent. Half of the subjects of my study left positions or sought new positions due to an ethical challenge they could not resolve. You might think of this as "choosing the hill to die on." What does your exit card say and what would you do next if you had to use it?

One measure of leadership effectiveness is the degree to which the long-term success of the organization is ensured. This measure of leadership effectiveness is not evident during the yearly performance review process but is reflected over time. The subject of the next chapter is the practice of leadership. It takes discipline, patience, and concentration to ensure that you and your organization thrive and survive over time.

NOTES

1. Ian Mitroff, *Managing Crises before They Happen* (New York: American Management Association, 2001), 7.
2. See Mitroff, *Managing Crises*, 34–35, for a list of the different types of crises and their risks.
3. See Mitroff, *Managing Crises*, 6.
4. See Mitroff, *Managing Crises*, 102.
5. Robert Terry, *Seven Zones for Leadership: Acting Authentically in Stability and Chaos* (Palo Alto, Calif.: Davies-Black Publishing, 2001), 211.

CHAPTER 10

The Practice of Leadership

Just like love, lead is a verb.

CUTTING THE GORDIAN KNOT

The development and participation of more people in leadership expands what is possible and contributes to our future survival. We must take responsibility for the conditions in our lives that can't possibly be understood and managed without collective action. The narrow view of leadership as the province of only those with superhuman qualities excludes most of us and is far too limiting. As long as this old view prevails, only the truly brave and wise can rescue us! How many super leaders do you know?

Our desire for super leaders reveals more about us than about leaders and leadership. We long to be protected from difficult or threatening circumstances. We desire to solve our problems with the right amount of creativity and finesse rather than through sacrifice, collaboration, and collective effort. We want to escape complexity by seeking simplicity—sometimes that's even possible when we learn and work together. Waiting for an Alexander the Great to lead us by conquering our enemies and our fears is not really an option. The Gordian knot that ties us down must be released with a different sword—our collective intelligence.

What limits us is the idea that the models of leadership of the past will continue to be useful to us in the future. The "c" words of the past, command, control, and contain, are rapidly being replaced by the "e" words of the future, engage, envision, and empower. Like the challenge of the Gordian knot, most problems in our communities are unsolvable when they are viewed as problems, not opportunities for adaptation and change. The only way to work within complexity is to consider the parts and the whole simultaneously and collectively. This means inferring relationships and thinking in novel ways about the present and the future. It takes all of us.

HEROIC LEADERSHIP REVISED

There is a purpose, place, and opportunity for heroic leadership. We need to have hope and faith in the possibility and presence of heroic leaders without giving up on the idea that leadership includes us all. The view that leadership is a collective activity and the responsibility of the membership does not exclude the possibility of individual acts of heroism; it just hopes for that and more. We need heroes and heroines—ordinary and extraordinary people who do the work of community. They risk and achieve because they are motivated to serve and because "they cannot not do it."[1]

We need to encourage and support the potential for lives of commitment to the greater good. *Heroic leadership is a moral activity in service to others that affirms and transforms people and communities.* A revised definition of heroic leadership fits more closely with the concepts of courage, risk, and service for community. We need more heroic leadership as I have defined it and fewer campaigns that diminish our assets and future.

THE ART OF LOVING AND LEADING

Leadership, like love, is an activity that improves with practice. Erich Fromm, author of *The Art of Loving*, describes the path to mature love. "With regard to the art of loving, anyone who aspires to become a master in this art must begin by *practicing* discipline, concentration and patience through every phase of his life."[2] Fromm defines discipline as an aspect of one's whole life—putting all our efforts to develop our capacity to love. Concentration is the ability to be alone and reflect on our actions and also to be fully present with others. Patience requires us to expect that the art of loving and maturity takes time.

Mature leaders practice the art of leading with similar efforts. The practice of leadership is disciplined. It requires us to put our energy and commitment into learning and service. We learn about leadership through participation, example, study, experience, and reflection. Concentrating on others and just plain listening is another aspect of practicing leadership. Leadership is primarily about the relationships we have with ourselves and each other. Communication fuels these relationships and is at the center of leadership.

There isn't any way to escape the commitment and concentration required to authentically participate in leadership—it takes more from us than we may be prepared to give. Patient leaders make strategic moves after research and reflection instead of rushing to action. The practice of leadership, like love, is a form of apprenticeship in relationships.

We need to have "crucial conversations" with each other in the spirit of inquiry and dialogue to explore how we can talk about leadership and develop a new understanding about our roles and relationships in leadership.[3] Crucial conversations are those that are occur when the stakes are high, strong emotions are involved, and there are a variety of opinions. I challenge you to participate in a crucial conversation about leadership, sharing with others what you think it is, seeking an understanding about what we all need from leaders and leadership, and taking on your share of the leader's work in the future.

Many define the crisis of leadership as the absence of capable leaders in our communities. I think this view is mostly incorrect. The real crisis of leadership is our lack of imagination and concern regarding how we can develop the collective potential for leadership among us. *The Elements of Leadership* can help you start the conversation—the rest is up to you.

In closing, I leave you with the words of Mary McLeod Bethune (1875–1955) as a gift to your spirit and leadership:

> I leave you love. I leave you hope. I leave you the challenge of developing confidence in one another. I leave you a thirst for education. I leave you responsibility for the use of power. I leave you faith. I leave you racial dignity. I leave you a desire to live harmoniously with your fellow man. I leave you a responsibility to our young people.[4]

NOTES

1. Laurent A. Park Daloz et al., *Common Fire: Leading Lives of Commitment in a Complex World* (Boston: Beacon Press, 1996), 197.

2. Erich Fromm, *The Art of Loving* (New York: Bantam Books, 1956), 93.

3. Kerry Patterson et al., *Crucial Conversation: Tools for Talking When the Stakes Are High* (New York: McGraw-Hill, 2002), 16.

4. Daloz et al., *Common Fire*, 81.

References

Bandura, Albert. *Self-Efficacy: The Exercise of Control.* New York: W. H. Freeman & Company, 1997.

Bass, Bernard. *Bass & Stogdill's Handbook of Leadership: Theory, Research, and Managerial Applications,* 3rd ed. New York: The Free Press, 1990.

Bennis, Warren, and Burt Nanus. *Leaders: The Strategies for Taking Charge.* Harper & Row Publishers, 1985.

Block, Peter. *Stewardship: Choosing Service over Self-Interest.* San Francisco: Berrett-Koehler Publishers, 1993.

Bolman, Lee, and Terrence Deal. *Reframing Organizations: Artistry, Choice, and Leadership.* 2nd ed. San Francisco: Jossey-Bass, 1997.

Bridges, William. *Managing Transitions: Making the Most of Change.* Reading, Mass: Addison-Wesley Publishing Company, 1991.

Buckingham, Marcus, and Don Clifton. *Now, Discover Your Strengths.* New York: Free Press, 2001.

Burbules, Nicholas C. *Dialogue in Teaching: Theory and Practice.* New York: Teachers College Press, 1993.

Capra, Fritjof. *The Web of Life: A New Scientific Understanding of Living Systems.* New York: Bantam Doubleday Dell Publishing Group, 1996.

Cleveland, Harlan. *Nobody in Charge: Essay on the Future of Leadership.* San Francisco: Jossey-Bass, 2002.

Clifton, Donald, and Paula Nelson. *Soar with Your Strengths.* New York: Dell Publishing, 1992.

Conger, Jay A. and associates, *Spirit at Work.* San Francisco: Jossey-Bass, 1994.

Cooperrider, David L, Peter F. Sorensen Jr., Diana Whitney, and Therese Yaeger, eds. *Appreciative Inquiry: Rethinking Human Organization toward a Positive Theory of Change.* Champaign, Illinois: Stipes Publishing L.L.C, 2000.

Daloz, Laurent A. Park, Cheryl H. Keen, James P. Keen, and Sharon Park Daloz. *Common Fire: Leading Lives of Commitment in a Complex World.* Boston: Beacon Press, 1996.

Dempsey, Jan. "MIT breaks new ground by offering free online courses," in the *Minneapolis Star Tribune*, November 12, 2002, E9.

De Pree, Max. *Leading without Power: Finding Hope in Serving Community.* San Francisco: Jossey-Bass, 1997.

Fromm, Erich. *The Art of Loving.* New York: Bantam Books, 1956.

Fullan, Michael. *Leading in a Culture of Change.* San Francisco: Jossey-Bass, 2001.

Goffman, Erving. *Frame Analysis: An Essay on the Organization of Experience.* New York: Harper & Row Publishers, 1974.

Greenleaf, Robert. *Servant Leadership: A Journey into the Nature of Legitimate Power and Greatness.* New York: Paulist Press, 1977.

Heifetz, Ronald A. and Marty Linsky. *Leadership on the Line: Staying Alive through the Dangers of Leading.* Boston, Harvard Business School Press, 2002.

Heifetz, Ronald A. *Leadership without Easy Answers.* Cambridge, Mass: Harvard University Press, 1994.

James, Jennifer. *Thinking in the Future Tense: Leadership Skills for a New Age.* New York: Simon & Schuster, 1996.

Jaworski, Joseph. *Synchronicity: The Inner Path of Leadership.* San Francisco: Berrett-Koehler Publishers, 1998.

Johnson, David W., and Frank P. Johnson. *Joining Together: Group Theory and Group Skills.* Boston: Allyn and Bacon, 2000.

Kelley, Robert E. *The Power of Followership: How to Create Leaders People Want.* New York: Bantam Doubleday Dell Publishing, 1992.

Kotter, John P. *John P. Kotter on What Leaders Really Do.* Boston: Harvard Business School Press, 1999.

Kouzes, James M., and Barry Z. Posner. *Credibility: How Leaders Gain and Lose It, Why People Demand It.* San Francisco: Jossey-Bass, 1993.

Lawrence-Lightfoot, Sarah. *Respect: An Exploration.* Reading, Mass: Perseus Books, 1999.

Maister, David M. *True Professionalism: The Courage to Care about Your People, Your Clients and Your Career.* New York: Touchstone, 1997.

Maranháo, Tullio, ed. *The Interpretation of Dialogue.* Chicago: University of Chicago Press, 1990.

McDowell, Banks. *Ethical Conduct and the Professional's Dilemma.* New York: Quorum Books, 1991.

Mitroff, Ian. *Managing Crises before They Happen*. New York: American Management Association, 2001.

Moxley, Russ S. *Leadership and Spirit: Breathing New Vitality and Energy into Individuals and Organizations*. San Francisco: Jossey-Bass, 2000.

Nanus, Burt. *Visionary Leadership: Creating a Compelling Sense of Direction for Your Organization*. San Francisco: Jossey-Bass, 1992.

Palmer, Parker J. *The Active Life: A Spirituality of Work, Creativity, and Caring*. San Francisco: Jossey-Bass, 1990.

Patterson, Kerry, Joseph Grenny, Ron McMillan, and Al Switzler. *Crucial Conversation: Tools for Talking When the Stakes Are High*. New York: McGraw-Hill, 2002.

Prince, George M. *The Practice of Creativity*. New York: Collier Books, 1970.

Schein, Edgar H. *Organizational Culture and Leadership*. 2nd ed. San Francisco: Jossey-Bass, 1992.

Senge, Peter M. *The Fifth Discipline: The Art and Practice of the Learning Organization*. New York: Doubleday Currency, 1990.

Senge, Peter, Nelda Cambron-McCabe, Timothy Lucas, Bryan Smith, Janis Dutton, and Art Kleiner. *Schools That Learn: A Fifth Discipline Fieldbook for Educators, Parents, and Everyone Who Cares about Education*. New York: Doubleday Dell Publishing Group, 2000.

Smith, Sarah J. "Women Administrators: Concepts of Leadership, Power, and Ethics," (Ed.D. dissertation, University of Wyoming, 1996.

Stanoch, Pam Pappas. "Carrying Cultural Baggage." *Northwest Airlines World Traveler*, January 2001.

Tennant, Mark, and Philip Pogson. *Learning and Change in the Adult Years*. San Francisco: Jossey-Bass, 1995.

Terry, Robert. *Seven Zones for Leadership: Acting Authentically in Stability and Chaos*. Palo Alto, Calif.: Davies-Black Publishing, 2001.

Toffler, Alvin. *Future Shock*. New York: Random House, 1970.

Willliamson, Marianne, ed. *Imagine What America Could Be in the 21st Century: Visions of a Better Future from Leading American Thinkers*. New York: New American Library, 2000.

Index

About the Author

Dr. Sarah J. Noonan is an associate professor of educational leadership at the University of St. Thomas in St. Paul, Minnesota, and teaches graduate-level classes in leadership and educational administration. Noonan previously served as a superintendent of schools for the School District of River Falls in River Falls, Wisconsin, and Teton County Schools in Jackson, Wyoming. She has also held a variety of other leadership positions, including assistant superintendent of schools, curriculum director, program specialist for a state department of education, and director of gifted education. Noonan consults in the areas of leadership development and executive coaching, personnel, change management, strategic planning, and board/superintendent development. She had fifteen years' experience as a classroom teacher prior to assuming administrative roles. Noonan's e-mail is sjnoonan@stthomas.edu.